To Radha,

You are an inspiration
to talk to.
I hope this book will be
life-changing for you!

Blessing,
Loretta

GET THE
GOOD
OUT OF
LIFE

GET THE GOOD OUT OF LIFE

Extracting the Good From Every Circumstance of Life

Loretta R. McIntosh

Glory Publications
Frisco, Texas

Printed in the United States of America.
ISBN 978-0-578-03843-8

Library of Congress Cataloging-in-Publication Data
McIntosh, Loretta R.
  Get the good out of life: extracting the good from every circumstance of life / Loretta R. McIntosh.
    p. cm.
  Includes some bibliographical references and resources.

ISBN 978-0-578-03843-8 (hardcover, jacketed)
1. Inspirational (Self-help). 2. Failure. 3. Recovery/Success. I. Title.

2014930104

Published in the United States by Glory Publications
5729 Lebanon Rd., Ste. 144-248, Frisco, Texas 75034
Visit our website at www.getthegoodoutoflife.com
Cover design: Glory Publications

Unless otherwise indicated, Scriptures are taken from the New Living Translation (NTL), copyright 1996, 2004. Used by permission of Tyndale House Publishers, Inc., Wheaton, Illinois 60189. All rights reserved.

Also used: The New King James Version® (NKJV). Copyright © 1982 by Thomas Nelson, Inc. Used by permission. All rights reserved.

The thought-provoking stories told and names mentioned in this book are used for the purpose of edification and encouragement and with permission granted. Last names, and in one case, first names are omitted to protect their privacy. And most importantly, my respect goes to the dearly departed that are mentioned in this book, as well as my love and sincere gratitude to their families. Our lives will be forever changed because of your kindness. Thank you!

Notes: any articles, books, and Internet addresses (websites, blogs, etc.) or their information in this book are offered as a resource. The information contained is not intended in any way to be an endorsement by the author or Glory Publications, nor do they vouch for the content of these sites for the life of this book.

In loving memory

of my mother and father,

Vernita & John

CONTENTS

To Christa

INTRODUCTION

I have discovered that in everything that we face— in all life's struggles, setbacks, disappointments, and even traumas—there is always that hidden element of good. Yet some people choose to accept defeat by dwelling on their past hurts and failures. And consequently, some of those same people will never advance out of their pit of despair.

Well, just as the powers of nature (water, air, and fire) all coexist with the earth, so does good with bad. This life produces both. Each one of these substances has the power to contribute to major disasters, or to meeting our basic and essential needs. Understand that the good and the bad things that happen in life exist in mutual tolerance of one another while in their season of operation. However, when the Laws of nature are violated, there remains no tolerance—only conflict. Perhaps natural, universal, and spiritual Law-breaking is the main reason why bad things happen to "good people," which in turn causes good things to happen to "bad people." But this book really isn't about what happens to "good or bad people." It's about extricating the good out of every situation in life—past, present, and future.

I know firsthand what it means to fail miserably in some areas of life; however, I managed to bounce back, and am now able to effectively help others. After many years of life coach training, and countless hours spent interviewing people, what stands out the most to me is the fact that we all have the same things in common: pain and human suffering.

Let's face it. We live in a broken world, and sometimes

life hurts! However, we all must understand that life's greatest lessons derive from our greatest failures, hurts, and losses. And since we can do absolutely nothing to prevent what we sometimes face, and since everything happens for a reason, we might as well locate the *good* reason for it and learn from it. And then allow that *good* reason to dominate every circumstance, which will ultimately navigate us to the positive side of life's challenges.

Remember, nothing bad ever happens without good being present, which gives you the power to choose the outcome of whatever happens to you—VICTORY or defeat!

Loretta R. McIntosh

CHAPTER 1

THE MIND TRAP

Many years had quickly passed, but Nicole's mentality and lifestyle still reflected the abandonment by both her mother and father and the rejection of being raised in an orphanage. It also reflected the pain of many years of promiscuity and drug use, as well as the trauma of her domestic abuse and divorce. As a result of her traumatization, Nicole's past had fashioned her character and personality, which ultimately affected every aspect of her adult life. It seemed as though everything went wrong for her, time and time again.

Nicole began telling herself that life was too short, and obviously too complicated, not to at least try to enjoy it. One day she decided to reinvent herself. This new self-help reinvention consisted of acquiring the finest material things that money could buy: an expensive new car, a high-rise apartment (overlooking the lake), the latest fashions, and a complete make-over of her appearance. Therefore, she constantly had a plethora of romantic possibilities. Nicole became an entirely different person when she dressed up. Everything she wore made a statement. But as time progressed, those who were close to her began to notice a very disturbing behavioral pattern.

Her co-workers, friends, and family all concluded that she had multiple personalities and Post Traumatic Stress Disorder (PTSD)! "But we all thought Nicole was a Christian," one co-worker said. Well, she was, in fact, a Christian, but she was still enslaved mentally to her past. Dressing up in her expensive designer clothes simply triggered her fantasies (unrestricted journeys of the imagination) of who she always desired to become.

Nicole wrote her own screen-play and acted out every character. This is how she avoided reliving her painful past on a daily basis. However, what Nicole and those who knew her failed to realize is that *the mind is a very powerful command center that controls everything;* and *the mind trap* victim is a trapped soul who is a prisoner in his or her own mind. Without *embracing change* mentally, nothing they do to change outwardly can alter that. Even possessing wealth won't bring that person true joy, peace, and happiness. And thus, all trapped souls of the mind believe that once a victim, always a victim! This is sad, but so very true—without the life-changing intervention of God.

I've met so many interesting people with such great potential who were trapped in the past yet desired to be free, but found no way to escape. *Enjoying the journey of life* is virtually impossible without a changed mind-set. When prison doors open, and it's time to begin *prioritizing life,* victims of their past, who are mental convicts, either stay inside or return after leaving for an instant. And some tend to experience fear from even the thought of what's beyond those prison doors. Why is this so? It is simply because remaining inside a familiar place or returning there, no matter how dangerous it may be, is a delusional comfort zone. This is the result of being locked into a negative mind-set, which is the number one cause of all relapses. But remaining in a comfort zone causes life to pass you by. Once you stay in a life of bondage that's filled with chaos for so long, it's hard to conceive getting *order out of chaos.* And once you've been traumatized and put in a mental prison like Nicole, it's hard to visualize anything else — except being in a cell and being around people who think like you do. And likewise, it's hard to comprehend the purpose for *extracting the good* from so much pain. Sometimes people mentally accept all the bad things that happen to them, supposing that they must have been at fault. And some suppose that their sins are too great for God and others to forgive, and that apparently, He must be punishing them. Consequently, they live life, but they remain robbed of *living the good life.* The trauma that Nicole experienced in a short period of time, most people don't experience in a life-time. Her pernicious blows in life were all stored in her subconscious mind, and subsequently influenced her actions.

Nicole's temporary fulfillment from the accumulation of her material things was simply used to veil her unhappiness; however, this is not what *experiencing the abundant life* is all about. The thought and implementation of reinventing herself was good; in fact, it's the first step to take after being emotionally healed, but nonetheless, what she really needed to experience in life was *the authentic good.*

Such hardships in life are designed to imprison and to utterly destroy. But we must always remember that the price for our freedom has been paid, and our freedom is now a choice. A final way of escape has been provided by the true Righteous Judge, who long ago granted us clemency.

The Mind-Set

The mind-set is a fixed mental attitude that influences a person's interpretation of things and how they respond to situations.

The Negative Mind-Set

Nothing good ever comes out of dwelling on the past, either negative or positive. Only hurt and stagnation can come from this. Anyone desiring to move forward in order to enjoy a better life must release their past and all forms of negativity associated with it, just like letting go of something extremely hot, like fire. If not, they are sure to be burned and perhaps scarred for life. The word negative expresses denial, refusal, or prohibition. It also implies subtraction. A good example of a person with a negative mind-set is a pessimist, for whom everything is always half this and not enough of that. Having this kind of person in your life will result in loss, nothing but loss.

Additionally, people with a negative mind-set live

in denial of their past, yet they relive it when under pressure, when upset, and when unable to cope with life's ups and downs. This is one of the reasons for broken relationships, failed marriages, and premature deaths. There are far too many past failures that become interpersonal conflicts in new relationships, all due to the constant rehearsals of past hurt. Conflicts also result from people living in denial of who they have become (products of their past environment), as well as denying that they need help.

Lee was a Vietnam veteran who returned from the war with PTSD, and later became a chronic alcoholic. To him, life was a party, and drinking alcohol was his way of escaping life's problems. On numerous occasions, Lee's family would arrive home to find him drunk and indecent or with his face collapsed into his plate of food. His favorite saying, "A little dab will do ya," referring to the numerous times he would reach for a bottle of alcohol, is the line he always used when questioned about his drinking problem. The biggest, brightest smile would cover his face whenever he verbalized this.

However, Lee's *negative mind-set*, which was covered up by his beautiful smile, kept him in denial for many years, and instead of believing the truth—a little dab will kill ya—he chose to believe a lie. After a decade of heavy drinking, he developed cirrhosis of the liver and died a very horrible death. This is proof that what you think and speak will govern your actions and steer the course of your life—all the way to the end of your life.

The Positive Mind-Set

You have the power (ability) to transform your way of thinking by renewing your mind with only positive, uplifting audiovisuals, literature, and biblical input. The word positive implies being optimistic, tending toward increase or progress.

A realistic illustration of a person with a positive mind-set is an optimist. An optimist always thinks and sees things differently, such as the glass is half full, and I'm not too far from the finish line. Establishing a relationship with this kind of person will help you to fulfill your purpose in life and will help catapult you into your destiny.

You should steer clear of all negative, ungodly, and corrupt communications—especially gossip—that are presented to you, which are as deadly as venomous snake-bites. And guard what you allow your mouth to speak and your eyes to see, also, because all of these vices will influence the way you think. Eventually they will impair your purpose vision.

Visualize your mind being like a computer: the computer is not all wise—the programmer is. *Whatever you download and meditate on (program your mind to think), that's what you will get out of life.* You are what you think! It's just that simple. When the enemies of your soul and the hindering forces of your future downloads the shameful things of your past, then pulls them up to condemn you, simply click DELETE, EMPTY TRASH, and then ERASE THE HISTORY!!! Change your old way of thinking to a *positive mind-set,* and you change the quality of your life.

The Achiever's Mind-Set

The achiever starts out with the mind-set that reaches forth and obtains the gold. And without any restraints the achiever goes beyond *average* and always strives for *excellence.* The achiever expects to succeed and therefore runs a race to win it—against all odds. An achiever is a high-flyer, one who creates his or her own success stories by executing plans. When choosing companions, the achiever seeks out and surrounds him or herself with conquerors that have defeated their own Goliaths in life.

This new breed person of excellence sees the outcome of total victory from the very beginning and will not accept anything less. An achiever often gleans from the wisdom and knowledge of others, and then implements and builds on a foundation of what's been tried and tested, believing that what others have accomplished, they can overachieve.

It doesn't matter how great the task that lies ahead, in the creative mind-set of the visionary achiever, nothing is impossible. And it doesn't matter how great the achiever's past failures and losses might be—the past is used as a platform on which to build.

This mind-set is in complete contrast to *the mind trap* (mental convict) way of thinking. Unequivocally, what you think, you envision; what you envision, you expect; and what you expect, you will possess. We should develop *the achiever's mind-set*, because too often our limitations come from our vision expectations.

CHAPTER 2

EMBRACING CHANGE

Thisis is the appointed time for you to accept and engage in your rite of passage, the one sure way of moving on to the next stage of life. In this case, the only ritual that's required is the renewing of your mind by gaining wisdom and knowledge of the truth that concerns you. The rite of passage milestones include various transitions from puberty, marriage, and death. And of course, there are the initiation ceremonies such as a baptism, a confirmation, and a Bar or Bat Mitzvah. All are considered important rites of passage for people of their respective faiths.

Transitioning from one state of mind, one position in life, or one level of growth to another is as easy as opening and closing your eyes. To do so, two main things are required of you: your willingness to change, and your obedience to the control center which is your brain, that sends you the signal to blink your eyes, to move your body, and to desire change. A housewife once stated that she believed that her husband was brain-dead. When asked why she believed that, she said, "Because every time I tell him to do something, he ignores me and nothing ever gets done." This is typical of the person who thinks that they are your control center. But only your control center can initiate the change. When you *hope* for a better life, your hope will eventually develop into faith, and your faith will emphatically trigger your willingness and obedience to do something about it. "If you are willing and obedient, you shall eat the good of the land" (Isaiah 1:19).

Prepare for your next dimensional change in life as you would for a graduation. Think of how long you've been in your holding place, and then say, "Today, I'm leaving this place of learning—what life has taught me throughout the years—and moving on!" Just hearing the word graduation gets me all excited about change. To me it means progress in motion—advancement and continued learning, if you will. It reminds you of the many years spent in solitary confinement, which includes all the hard work, studying, tests, trials, tribulation, opposition, and accumulated debt. And then afterwards, you enjoy the freedom from it all and the implementation of what you've learned. Your graduation not only validates all of your impressive achievements in life, but it also publicly reveals your ability to endure hardship along the way. This, in turn, will release you to leave your imprint on society—the indelible mark of who you really are. Remember, *exceptional people always emerge from great adversity.* No one achieves anything without going through—and successfully passing—the test of endurance. In every life there will be some rain. But instead of you failing yet another course—due to the enormous amount of pressure that you faced, and your lack of understanding the purpose for your pain—you stayed the course, received your degree and moved on up to higher learning. You now have wisdom and knowledge from what your past life lessons have taught you; and since knowledge is power, and "wisdom is the principle thing" that builds its house, I'm sure you will concur that the immense price you had to pay was worth it all!

Sharon was in her fifties when she realized that half a century had passed her by and all she had to show for it were the things she had accomplished for other people. She was gifted and talented, and operated in the spirit of excellence when helping and working for others. But there was one thing that held her back from doing great feats and receiving accolades of her own. It was the residue of the verbal and emotional abuse of her late husband in a marriage of thirty years. Sharon spent all those years listening to the man she loved say things like, "You are dead weight, overweight, crazy, and stupid!" All too often, he would withhold his affection from her, as well sexual intimacy. To be sure, this created a mind-set of inadequacy and rejection in Sharon.

One day while going through her late husband's chest, Sharon found a locked metal box with a key taped to the bottom of it. And on the top of the box there was a message written in black that read, "KEEP OUT!" So, out of curiosity, she opened the box and found a sealed envelope that read, "Don't open until I'm dead!" Apparently, all the negative word curses that her husband spoke over her had now returned to sender. He saw his own death and was prepared for it. Sharon began to weep softly and trembled as she slowly tore open the envelope. She looked inside and found a note that read,

> *I really did try to love you, Sharon, but the painful abuse of my childhood always kept standing in the way of my loving you. Whenever I looked at you, for some strange reason, I saw the face of my mother, who verbally and physically abused me and caused me so much pain. I'm sorry for all the pain I caused you throughout all those years. Please forgive me for the damage that was done. Please know that YOU ARE THE BEST THING THAT'S EVER HAPPENED TO ME!*
>
> *Love, Billy*

Sharon continued to live with a man who mistreated her because she understood that *when people get hurt, they shut down and they do to others what's been done to them.* However, Billy's words of love and redemption brought total healing to the damaged emotions of a woman who was bound by negative words of abuse for over thirty years. How disturbing it was for Billy, due to his obstinacy, to die this way without hope. In addition, Sharon's insecure mind-set was changed in an instant as the power of those words swept over her soul. At this point, she wiped away her tears, let go of her pain, and began embracing change. "To console those who mourn in Zion, to give them beauty for ashes, the oil of joy for mourning, the garment of praise for the spirit of heaviness…" (Isaiah 61:3).

At fifty-eight, Sharon graduated with honors from her local college. A few years later, she went on to become the first female president of the company she worked for. To Sharon, her greatest accolade in life was her ability to forgive and love someone wounded, who needed unconditional love and forgiveness. A metamorphosis is what must take place when your character and the poor conditions of your life are corrupting and imprisoning you.

But experiencing change is only inevitable to those who understand and accept the process of elimination. To discover the power of change you have to eliminate (assassinate) the reputation of your past in your mind. In other words, you must do away with the memory of bad conduct, which consists of things you used to say or do, or perhaps things that were said or done to you. And in some cases, this means excluding the people who caused your greatest pain. This is paramount! To understand the flow of life's changes, you must recall the functions of the human anatomy.

Imagine your body ingesting food only and never releasing, and then imagine your life ingesting pain and suffering only and never releasing. When you ingest food or liquids your body breaks down all the nutrients, vitamins, etc., and releases them to where they are most needed, and what's left is waste material. Your body then goes through what is called the process of elimination, which removes the waste matter to keep you healthy and free from all toxins, free radicals, etc. Now, if the body doesn't release itself daily, then medical help should be sought after. Obviously, there's a problem. Failure to eliminate fecal matter is one of the main causes for bloating and the all-American "muffin top" appearance of many people. And I must also mention the other causes for bloating: overeating, consuming junk food/ comfort food, and poor exercise. Life is the same way. The good, the bad, and everything in between have all been allowed into our lives for a reason, but when it's time for the bad things to be released, you will sense it and know that it's your time for change (elimination). However, without elimination, the buildup will affect every aspect of your life and the people around you.

Don't allow any more valuable time to pass without diagnosing the problems you're facing. If you are honest with yourself and are ready to confront the real issues in your relationships, marriage, finances, business, social and spiritual life, etc., then the elimination process will be child's play. I help people all the time, by way of instructing, lecturing, life coaching, mentorship, and through my literary work and have witnessed firsthand what a buildup of silent pain can do. So many people allow what they go through to weigh heavily on them for years, without exercising the right to reject the hurt that repeatedly comes to them. And like stored fat in the body, their silent pain and secret sins all develop into physical and emotional health problems. Suffice it to say, change on this level requires immediate confrontation, because the detrimental warning signs demands it.

Kim was a very hard working young woman who had become extremely successful in her law practice. She was single with no children due to her hectic schedule. But after years of growing her law firm, she realized that having a lot of money, as well as having so much freedom in her personal life, left her empty. Kim was attractive, highly intelligent, and well-suited to meet a person of her caliber.

While she was vacationing in the Florida Keys, she met a medical doctor who had a practice in her hometown. They later married and had aspirations of starting a family. Year after year they tried to have a baby, but to no avail. So naturally, Kim's husband David suggested that they both get checked out in hopes of finding the cause of the problem. David, a health nut, had spent many years eating right, exercising, and taking excellent care of his body, and had a physique to prove it. But so had Kim; she was his equal. When the reports of their medical conditions came back, they revealed that both Kim and David were in tip-top physical shape. After reviewing the report, David said to Kim, "Perhaps the problem is stress related." "But I'm not under a lot of stress, at least not enough to cause this problem," Kim replied.

Later, Kim found out that the problem was with her and that her problem was emotionally internal. At the age of thirteen, Kim was sexually violated and exposed to pornography by a boy in high school. Growing up, she never told a soul, not even her loving family. The fear of this one day happening to one of her children plagued her all the way to adulthood. It was the silent emotional pain that was blocking her conception. "There is no fear in love; but perfect love casts out fear, because fear involves torment…" (I John 4:18). The wounded side of her really didn't want any children, especially an innocent little girl. Always remember, a successful life is designed to flow like a river that is unblocked, and with this unhindered movement comes a constant change of scenery as you enter each phase of life. Kim and David both experienced the scenery of success and wealth on one level, but due to an emotional blockage of past pain and fear, they lived void of enjoying the beautiful scenery of parenthood on another level.

CHAPTER 3

ENJOYING THE JOURNEY

OF LIFE

A century of living consists of four quarters, or seasons, of life. Most healthy people will live through an entire century, while a few others may live past a century. Life is a journey, and from the beginning to the end, the journey will be experienced six different ways: as an excursion, an expedition, a jaunt, a pilgrimage, a trip, and a voyage. All of these words refer to a course of travel to a particular destination, usually for a specific purpose. However, there are many distinct differences between each of them.

A journey implies traveling for a very long time and distance over land. An *excursion* is a short trip involving pleasure that returns to its departure place. An *expedition* is an organized journey that takes place for a specific purpose. A *jaunt* is a brief, casual trip that's designed for enjoyment. A *pilgrimage*, of course, indicates a journey to a place of religious significance. A *trip*, whether long or short, business or pleasure, is often taken when the need arises, or at leisure. And finally, a *voyage* is a long, extended trip through air or by water.

Why is this important for us to know? It's important because the comfort or discomfort that you experience on your journey of life is predicated on your method of travel, and your method of travel is symbolic of the everyday choices you make. Instead of turning right, you chose to turn left, and turning left was the wrong choice. Understanding this simple metaphor will help you to see why there are so many consequential detours, changes, disappointments, and setbacks in life. The travel choices you make and the travel courses you take will effect how you live your life, as well as influence the final outcome of it. Additionally, the journey of life is seasonal, and there are insightful parallels between the changes of life and the changing seasons of nature. "To everything there is a season, a time for every purpose..." (Ecclesiastes 3:1).

The First Quarter of Life

The *first quarter* of life reflects *spring*: a time of learning, the years of growth and development. (The period of life that takes twenty-five years from birth for the brain to develop.) A very important part of this season consists of the primary years that exposes children to our world, and prepare them to become active participants in this life-long journey of learning. It's also a time of giving birth to something, and a time of discovery. It's the time when life begins to blossom and reveal who we are and what we are becoming. And it's the period of puberty and spiritual awareness.

This reminds me of an adolescent boy who finally

reached *puberty*. After he experienced this new stage of maturity, he called his mother one morning and said to her, "Hey, Mom, whatcha doing?"

"Good morning, son!" she replied, excited to hear his voice that early in the morning.

"Mom, guess what!?" he asked.

"What?" his mom replied.

Unashamedly and with a sigh of relief he said, "I just had a wet dream!"

"A what kind of dream!?"

"A wet dream, Mom!"

"You mean to tell me you've gone from wetting your pants to wetting your bed?"

"No ma'am, I..."

She interrupted him and said, "Well, that's good, because to become a man you need to be able to control your bladder in the daytime and at night, because they're both embarrassing, honey."

Mothers were not meant to be fathers, were they? Sometimes we simply do not understand. The spring season of life is often full of wonderful surprises, and is the awakening of many things. For many people this is their favorite time of the year, and the most carefree time of their lives.

Alexis had big dreams of becoming a pediatrician, and was extremely excited about going to college. She struggled with some of her courses during her freshman year of high school, but managed to graduate in spite of what others said. Plans had already been made for her to attend a college in the fall of the year of her graduation. When school started, she realized that she was stuck with a class she cared nothing about. However, this class began to incite a *spiritual awareness* in her. She never considered herself to be a religious person, but she did believe that there was "a God up there somewhere."

The professor stood before his class, gave them his name and began to instruct them. At first Alexis listened attentively, and then she withdrew herself from what he was saying. The professor concluded by saying, "If you are questioning if there really is a God, after today, you will question this no more." Alarmed by what she was hearing, she assumed that eventually he would say that there is indeed a God. The professor became evasive, and paused in the middle of his statement. Then he said, "Enough of that. Let's all get better acquainted."

Weeks of lecturing went by, and then finally the professor returned to his topic and declared, "I believe there is a god who lives in each one of us because you and I are little gods. Just think of the power we have at our disposal: through the power of medicine, we heal; through sexual intimacy, we create; through revenge, we kill; etc."

This subtle approach persuaded Alexis a little, and caused her to question her original belief. His doctrine made sense to her, and answered a lot of her questions. Before she knew it, she was telling others what she had been taught by her professor.

Alexis returned home a different person during the Christmas break. She had become arrogant, controlling and settled in her new belief about God. When her parents invited her to attend a Christmas cantata, she turned them down, thinking to herself, *Who needs to celebrate a God when you are one yourself?* Alexis isolated herself from her family to avoid any confrontation until she returned to school. She eventually dropped out of school and never completed her studies.

Obviously, Alexis was *falsely indoctrinated and turned from the truth.* Not only did it turn her away from God, it altered her entire life, because she embraced it. (Life lesson: closely observe what your children are being taught, and reach out and help them.) When we are very young, we are naïve and impressionable; but remember, this is the time of growth and cultivation and we must guard what we allow ourselves to see and hear. As we grow older we should seek to grow wiser with the *knowledge of the truth* in our spring season of life, and all seasons, for that matter.

The Second Quarter of Life

The *second quarter* of life reflects *summer*: a time of implementing what we've learned in spring, and a time when we strive to make our mark in life. This is a very active season of high adventure and bountifulness. It's actually a time to really enjoy life.

During this season we cease being dull and aloof, and we experience a strong desire to connect with family and friends, as well as a desire to belong to someone and to feel a part of something. We shed layers of our lives as we do clothing in the summer, and we open our hearts more to love. New relationships are developed as we enlarge our circle of friends.

It was a blistering-hot summer day at the beach in the Bahamas, and there he was, a gorgeous man with six-pack-abs. Monica glanced to her right and caught him staring at her. About ten minutes later he made his way over to her, and started a conversation with her. To her surprise, his personality didn't coincide with his good looks. He was soft-spoken, and appeared to be a humble and caring person. Instead of having wandering eyes that looked at, and lusted for, every woman on the beach, he was very attentive to her when she spoke. (Men who listen to women sometimes win with them right away.) (Life lesson: men, please learn to listen.)

Monica, who was forty years old and single, wasn't

bad-looking herself. In fact, she was beautiful, inside and out. This very attractive thirty-eight-year-old man named Carlos expressed to Monica that he had never been married, and that he definitely wasn't gay, but was simply waiting for the right woman to come along.

Carlos and Monica meshed and spent their entire vacation together and fell deeply in love with each other. They knew that this was more than a vacation romance. A week later they both returned to the States, and continued to see each other. Carlos was a successful banker, and Monica was a general practitioner. They were inseparable, and appeared to be meant for each other. The two of them had a lot in common, and worked together as a team to sort out their differences.

Months later, on a luxury cruise to Tahiti, Carlos proposed to Monica. But Monica burst into tears, left the dinner table and locked herself in her cabin. After Carlos calmed her down and questioned her, a well-kept secret was revealed. While warmly embraced by him, Monica emotionally said, "I've never lied to you about anything else except this one thing that's tormenting me!"

"And what is this one thing?" Carlos asked.

"Remember when we first met in the Bahamas and you said that I seemed a little distant?" Monica asked. Carlos nodded his head. "Well, the truth is, I had just ended a two-year relationship with a guy, and I was there because I needed some time away from everyone. Carlos, I'm pregnant! We both know it's not your child because we haven't slept together. There's only one person who could be the father, and it's Jeff. I'm so sorry for this mistake! It must have happened the last time we were together. The reasons I didn't tell you sooner are that I just found out, and because I honestly and truly do not want to lose you! But, I do understand if you're hurt and never want to see me again."

Carlos remained silent for a while and dropped his head. Then he got down on one knee, took her by the hand and said, "Monica…, will you marry me?"

With many tears streaming down her cheeks, Monica said, "Yes!" and they were married days later after they arrived on Bora Bora Island.

Perhaps it's once in a life-time that true love will

find you, as it did Monica. Stay hopeful, and be sure not to settle for less! You'll know it when it happens. Sometimes the season of summer begins and ends with an unprecedented *blast!*

The Third Quarter of Life

The *third quarter* of life reflects *fall*: a time of change and reciprocation: exchange, giving back, and the reaping of the fruit of your labor. This season of modification brings closure to many things. While experiencing this closure, we also witness the beauty of the changing colors of fall.

Be mindful of the fact that this season also interrupts many marriages due to a couple's lack of understanding the pause of life's physical reproduction. Husbands are often driven away when unable to cope with their mate's hormonal changes and deficiencies. Wives find it difficult to cope with their mates who are struggling with their mid-life crisis, and perhaps their desire for younger women. Truthfully, this season of your life will require every ounce of *courage, hope, faith, stamina, endurance, steadfastness, forgiveness, trust, patience, and unwavering love* that you have to make it through the emotional turbulence.

Tim and his wife Cindy were both in their late fifties when their lives suddenly changed. In the beginning Tim was very confused about what was happening to his wife, until he began to study her behavior and seek help. Years went by, and things got worse instead of better. One Saturday morning, while contemplating whether to leave Cindy or to stay and continue to suffer emotionally, Tim knelt down and began to weep and to pray. Out of anguish he expressed himself through many complaints. After a while he experienced a gentle calm and a peace that flooded his entire being. A few hours later, Tim called a confidant and said, "You know... I love my wife. She's the love of my life. But she is intolerable to live with, and today I had planned to end it all! While in prayer this morning something happened to me, and for the first time I now understand why my strong, fun-loving wife has become a fragile, disturbed woman who seems to have no control over her life anymore. I realize that she is not my enemy. What I've witnessed is painful enough for me to honestly say, *I cannot leave her in the state she's in."*

It is true that prayer changes things, and during this unpredictable third quarter of life it will require much prayer and a lot of dying to yourself to help the one you love. In this season it may seem as though you will be codependent for the rest of your life, but be at rest; things will get better with help and with time.

Furthermore, this is the season that reminds the baby boomers of the golden years to come. However, *this is not the time to retire, but to re-fire,* and to celebrate life. If you've succeeded in life and accomplished many things, then this is the time to enjoy them. You've paid your dues, and now you deserve to have life's best! In this season you are given the power to mend your broken and shattered life, and to experience some good times with those who understand what you may be going through.

It's okay to enter your fall season with reservations, because this is the season of the unknown. You may experience so many things that you're unsure of, and although each experience is so different and sometimes challenging, they are all important components of life. In the beginning of the fall season of life it ushers in a beautiful change, and then it fluctuates; however, this season is not only beautiful and mysterious, it's essential.

The Fourth Quarter of Life

The *fourth quarter* of life reflects *winter:* a time of arriving and settling in with a hot cup of mocha after your long journey of life. It's also a time to count your blessings as you reflect on your spring, your summer, and your fall seasons. This is also the season of hibernation, and for many people it's the time of releasing and letting go of their lives in total surrender to God.

This is the positive side of hibernation in winter that most people overlook. My beautiful grandmother was ninety-seven years young when she passed from her winter season in hibernation to heaven. She was only three years short of living to be one hundred. Whenever she made an entrance, her smile would light up the room. I still recall the many words of wisdom that she spoke, and the joy I felt each time I was in her presence. Sweet memories! Nothing but pure, sweet memories! All *hats off to sweet grandmothers* who exemplify the true meaning of love, and who help to build character in their grandchildren. You are the best!

Another positive side of hibernation is being able to rest and enjoy being *temporarily* inactive. Much like plants, you're still alive during this season, but you're just not budding and growing outwardly. Reaching this destination and experiencing optimum rewards in this winter season will be determined by everything you did and did not do in all the other seasons of your life.

Joe and Ella fell deeply in love, married young, and remained together for sixty years. They were the talk of the town, and pillars in their local church. Whenever the church doors opened they were there and ready to serve. Although they were retired from working, they remained active in their community.

One sad day, Ella became very ill and bedridden. She

became frail and unable to care for herself; but there was no impairment in her mental faculties. Ella was a very charitable individual who was cherished by so many of the people who knew her. When an acquaintance of hers (a retired nurse) received word that Ella was sick, she dropped everything that she was involved in and began tending to her. Four months went by, and Ella's humble acquaintance remained steadfast in caring for her. The following week, Ella became worse, and called her husband to her bedside.

She said, "Joe, I've discovered something wonderful about God. He never leaves us alone and hopeless, and when tested and asked to obey Him, He always provides a *ram in the bush!* Now, I know you know His voice, so what I'm about to say to you should ring true to you. The woman who is tending to me is your next wife after me."

"Ella, hush now! Don't talk like that!" Joe boldly replied.

With all the strength she could muster, Ella said, "Joe, listen to me. God is calling me home, but He wants you to stay a little while longer. This *angel* who lovingly nursed and served me all this time was *sent to us* by Him. Take your time grieving when I'm gone, and then marry her, Joe, marry her." And with her *last* breath she said, "I will always love you!"

Apparently, Ella's spiritual discernment and her last words resonated with Joe because only a short time passed before he married *Ella's angel*, whom he came to love in a special way. At age eighty, Joe experienced a new life and love once again.

The words we speak are very powerful. They always prevail with the listener, and likewise with the reader. The winter season is a gray, cold and shivery time of life, but it's also a time of *restoration* and *warm embrace.* Joe found the strength to release one person, and the grace to embrace another.

In summary, all of these predestined seasons have four divisions: spring brings *promise,* summer promotes good *success,* fall introduces *change,* and winter invites *re-discovery.* However, many circumstantial experiences of life will *alter* your seasons from time to time, and try to dictate to you which season you *must* operate in. Sometimes winter tries to enter in and dominate summer, causing you to experience a nonproductive, dry and low season. Spring will often try to rush in during winter, causing you to abort something or to give birth prematurely. Fall tries to interrupt spring, to prevent you from giving birth to something and to alter things that should be left alone. Then summer tries to overextend itself into fall, which always hinders change.

But you are the gatekeeper of your life, and what comes and goes is within your control. *Enjoying the journey of life* involves making decisions that positively effect all that you do and every road that you travel.

PRIORITIZING LIFE

What comes to mind when you think of the importance of prioritizing your life? The majority of people would begin by placing their spiritual life, people, and things in an order of precedence, such as God first, their family second, and then their employment. But if you look at this scenario, you'll find that something of value is missing here: you! Individual you! Prioritizing life begins with you.

I know this may sound selfish, but it's true. It's you who needs to be renewed daily in spirit, soul, and body in order to develop good, healthy relationships with

God, your family, and others. You cannot give out to other people what you don't have within yourself. And we all know that sometimes the demand to please other people is far greater than that to please God. But with this tall order of always pleasing people comes guaranteed failure. God will not be second to anyone or anything in your life.

A very devoted wife and mother spent long hours in prayer while her husband was at work and her children were at school. One day her youngest son, a six-year-old, faked a stomachache and was allowed to stay home for the day. Refusing to neglect her appointed time of prayer, the mother entered her prayer room and began to pray very softly. Her son in the other room began shouting, "Mom, I'm hearing strange voices! Please come and help me!"

His mother ignored his request for help and continued praying. Again, her son shouted the same words, except much louder than before. His mother left her prayer room and entered his bedroom and said, "Why are you shouting, and what did the voices say to you?"

The boy said, "I think this was God, Michael, and Gabriel telling me to tell you that I'm very hungry and need you to bring me some food to eat, because you were too busy talking to Him and not listening."

Sometimes the demands of our family life can be so overwhelming that they interrupt the flow of your "me" time, as well as your *devotional* time. But your well-being is equally as important as that of your loved ones and other people in your life right now. Both enhancing and maintaining who you are will cause those you love to reap greater dividends in their relations with you.

Life is both temporal and eternal. It's temporal while here on earth and it's eternal in the afterlife. This is why it's vitally important to prioritize the part of life (you) that is temporal, placing things of paramount importance first, and then all the rest, understanding that what happens to you in your eternal life will be the result of what took place in your temporal life. A sobering thought, isn't it? Since the human lifespan is short-lived like a vapor, and since you have but one life to live here on earth, you should place urgency on living and loving it. And you should also see it as God's gift for you to enjoy.

My way of prioritizing this temporal life is to put my relationship with God first and foremost, my need for growth and character development second, my family third, and my profession last. Albeit, I must candidly say, my life wasn't always this orderly. I missed it in the beginning, but now I have it right. Thankfully! Keeping this order enhances my ability to succeed in life and helps me to live a more fulfilling life—a non-frustrated, worry-free lifestyle—that's purposeful and faith-based. In the beginning years of my life and profession, I allowed too much valuable time to escape, while working my fingers to the bones: supporting, giving, teaching, mentoring, and helping everyone else to live the good life, without living the good life myself.

One morning I stopped and took an inventory of my life and began releasing the old stifling things that hindered my progress and made way for the new. You should imitate this, because this is the first step toward prioritizing life. It's true. The first step is cleaning house.

Make time for you now. And avoid being *stressed* out. It's funny that the word *stressed* spelled backwards is *desserts*. Maybe it's time for you to escape from all the cares of this life and simply enjoy your favorite beverage and *desserts* (the sweeter side of life).

Then perhaps after you've recovered a bit, you'll zealously start your own campaign, run for office, vote for yourself, and win! And then be sure to do your very best to successfully accomplish the rest of what's on your priority "to do" list. Seize every opportunity in life that God gives you, as if there will be no tomorrow, and let no persuasion or power deter you in your mandate.

In 1980, one of those golden opportunities of a life-time came my way. My plans were to start a business that would later develop into a chain of businesses. Everything was set and in place for me to move speedily ahead. Just minutes before I was to sign the contract, I heard this "still, small voice" say to me, "Will you take My healing to the nations?" I looked around and laughed, thinking that I had been in the sun too long, and now, I was starting to hear things. With haste, I continued walking to my car to avoid being late meeting my broker. I got inside my car and heard these same words again. By this time I was thinking, *This can't be what I think it is—coming from who I think it is!* So I boldly and facetiously responded by saying, "Sorry, but I'm not who you're looking for. I'm on my way to sign a business contract, right now!" Then, all of a sudden, I had an overwhelming urge to weep, and so I did, very softly and then quite profusely. I went from laughing to weeping. Never before or since have I experienced anything quite like this. I felt as though my irreverent rejection had canceled my future without even knowing what that future was. Immediately, I lost track of all time, and of course, I missed my appointment with a man (the broker) in exchange for a truly divine appointment with God. I tell you the truth; I have never been the same since that encounter.

However, out of ignorance, I continued to say no to this mandate and continued with business as usual, which a couple of weeks later almost cost me my life— literally! I had a car accident and was hit by an 18-wheeler and suffered severe injuries to my back and neck (the unbearable pain of pinched nerves and muscle spasms) but very little damages to my vehicle. Puzzling! Right!

This life lesson taught me the dangers of saying no to God simply because you don't know or understand who He really is. And although I didn't seize the opportunity, as I've instructed you to do, I did eventually say yes. And now, nearly thirty-four years later, I'm still saying yes and "taking healing to the nations" with medical supplies, food, clothing, literature, etc., and I have the potential to reach the masses in a much greater capacity via the Internet and television.

Saying yes also resulted in me being divinely healed of the severe back and neck injuries that I suffered. For years after being healed, I traveled to other countries that required me to sit on a plane for eleven or more hours, non-stop; I ran three to five miles a day; and I played tennis on a regular basis. And all of this was done without pain, and without having surgery or taking medication.

That which was trivial to me back then has now

become top priority in my life. Who would have thought that the one thing that I was born to do, and would spend my entire adult life doing, could have been forfeited in an instant?

Opportunities that bring us a better life, along with ways by which to help people, will come and go like a ticking clock. If you miss one minute of grasping them they will pass you by. Sadly, this almost happened to me—but try to avoid this happening to you.

Most Valuable and Precious

The things that are most costly to us are the things that fully occupy our hearts. When I meet a person, I always look for their treasures in order to locate their heart. If an individual tries to impress me with the material things that they possess, or if they speak excessively of their knowledge of God, I immediately discover where their heart is. "Wherever your treasure is, there the desires of your heart will also be" (Matthew 6:21).

We all should remember to prioritize storing up

things in heaven versus storing up things on earth; and we should also place our love for God and people above our lust for things. I've seen people weep and become chronically depressed over the foreclosure of a house, the repossession of a vehicle, or the loss of an animal; and then there are other people who celebrate after a divorce or rejoice at the loss of a family member who left an inheritance.

A divorce, for some people, simply separates their hatred of one another and gives them legal visitation rights to see their children when taken and isolated by the disgruntled parent. And for some people, the death of someone brings the long-awaited closure that they hoped for and needed. So, instead of feeling remorse or grief, they celebrate.

In these cases, it's very apparent that their priorities are placed only on possessing things, having provision, being comforted, and on having their insatiable desires met, rather than on what's *most valuable and precious:* sharing life and love with family and other people.

The Center of Everything

How could the center of everything be anything less than the core or vine of something, the one vital organ that pumps life-giving blood through our veins, and of course, the central nervous system? The truth is, *the center of everything* in life is the Creator of everything.

All things were created by Him and for Him; without Him at the center there can be no proper structure of life. Any wise person who reveres God and sees the absolute necessity for Him in the functioning of everyday life will inevitably live a successful and well-balanced life.

Family First

I believe the true meaning of putting your family first is hidden in the meanings of the words: covenant and commitment. A true *covenant* as we know it today is an agreement, both verbal and contractual. And *commitment* is the restriction of freedom to act contrary to a covenant that is made. When a marriage is sanctioned by God and there's no infidelity or abuse involved, it then becomes a covenant between Him, you, and your family. Metaphorically, your family becomes His family, and He will never consent to breaking His covenant by divorcing His family.

The willingness to remain committed to the marriage covenant is quite pleasing to Him and places a covering of protection over your entire family. Understanding this truth will help you to place your family's priorities in the order of significance:

1. Quality time spent with your mate (more so than other people, in-laws included).

2. Quality time spent with your children, both individually and collectively (more so than work or ministry).

3. Quality time spent with the family as a whole (more so than any other commitment).

4. Quality time spent with you alone (more so than anything or anyone else)!

Once you give your word to your family, keep it! If you break it in any way, you will sever their trust and ties with you and create a breach that often cannot be repaired. Keeping the *family first* means keeping the family together. And growing strong as a family requires more than what money can buy them, more than quality time spent with them, and even more than love itself—it requires commitment on everyone's part.

Why is commitment so paramount in our family relations? It's important because some people fall in and out of love very easily, and sometimes you don't always feel love for one another and that's when commitment is required. Perhaps you're thinking, *If commitment is of the utmost importance, then what part does "quality time spent" play in this?*

Quality time spent can also mean frustrated times together because these are the same people that you see and live with every day. Sometimes the people that you love the most, especially your family, can be the most irritating. But that's okay, invest the time anyway.

Additionally, and most importantly, there's a very

thin line between meeting your family's financial needs and buying their love. A wife, a husband, or children may be left with feelings of emptiness inside when given a major credit card, large amounts of cash, etc., to replace genuine love—or to replace you, for that matter. This is the result of a parent who fails to realize that having and releasing money doesn't make a family happy.

When children are given expensive material things at an early age, without working to acquire things on their own, they sometimes grow up deprived of having built good character. Yes, it's wonderful being able to give your children what you may or may not have had growing up. But consider this: it could only make life miserable for their future mate, who will one day live with the underdeveloped person you've created. Instead, prayerfully release them: to grow, to discover love, to make the right choices, to explore, to experience joy, to WORK (okay, you should be laughing right now; it's okay, you can thank me later), and even to make mistakes without crucifying them for being human.

So many young people today are living in beautiful

houses, driving exotic cars, wearing designer clothes—yet they're on drugs and alcohol, and in dire need of receiving help through counseling. I know this because they often come to me for help. Remember, it's better to have things and to do all things in moderation, and although some say moderation is for cowards, I say moderation is heroic.

The Place of Success

It has been said that if you really want to measure the degree of a man's success, look into the face of his wife. This face is what she has become as the result of his definition of success. If success to him meant neglect, infidelity, or any form of abuse, you will see it revealed in her face. The eyes and the countenance reflect the condition of the soul.

However, wives who are familiar with this statement try their best to camouflage it with laughter and a smile. And sometimes wives who are in denial of how unhappy they really are use the cover-ups of designer clothing and material things to give the appearance of inner joy and overwhelming success.

It's either your need or greed that drives you to succeed, but if a man's success is achieved out of greed rather than need, there will be consequences. This isn't success at all. "The blessing of the Lord makes a person rich, and he adds no sorrow with it" (Proverbs 10:22).

Success has its place. And when success is achieved while you're honoring God, enjoying and nurturing your family, establishing healthy new relationships, and maintaining your health, everyone benefits. *This is the place of success!* I guarantee you, a family that genuinely loves you would rather have you than the success that robbed them of you.

A successful couple who lived in the suburbs had just about everything that their money could buy. They both traveled extensively and very seldom saw their children, a fifteen-year-old boy and a twelve-year-old girl. One day their nanny reported that the son was missing after hours of waiting for him. Their daughter arrived home on time, and as usual, she isolated herself in her room. The nanny received a call stating that the boy had been hit by a car and died before he arrived at the hospital. The caller stated, "Apparently, the boy had taken a different route home and was using his cell to try and reach his dad to help resolve a problem he was facing. Instead of paying attention to the oncoming traffic, he was too engaged in making the call. He was struck and knocked several feet into the air. When the paramedics arrived, there was blood everywhere. While doing everything they could to save him, he died on the way to the hospital!" The couple returned home from their business meetings devastated and in complete shock, as the death of their son cast a dark shadow over their entire community.

Some people pay a high price for their success, which often leaves their families in total ruins. But they missed the entire purpose for their struggle. They may have finished, but they didn't finish strong. And they failed to realize that strength is built by one's failures, not one's successes. Their outcome, however, should have been lessons learned during the struggle, instead of *success at last,* along with family failure. I believe that acquiring money (the god of success) without balancing the rest of your life is ludicrous.

We must always differentiate between the true need (desire) for money and the love (lust) of money when seeking success. "For the love of money is the root of all kinds of evil. And some people, craving money, have wandered from the true faith and pierced themselves with many sorrows" (I Timothy 6:10).

And furthermore, another important thing for us to remember is that once success is achieved on any level— be it business, corporate, or ministerial—apart from personal success, the void inside causes some people to seek fulfillment (false hope and satisfaction) elsewhere. This generally occurs in marriages where dissatisfaction with a mate is used as a license for an extramarital affair or for walking away from their marriage partner altogether. How devastating the blow must be for their mate after years of support. But it doesn't matter what you've had to endure in this life, you should score everything under *experience* rather than *failure* or *defeat.*

When you prioritize you, God, your family, and then your success, you will reap the reciprocal benefits that the good life has to offer. And just as *prioritizing life* begins with you, it also ends with you. So start enjoying life to the fullest, but don't live life and lose your family. Don't make the costly mistake of living life and then arriving at the end of this life without your eternal security being in right standing with God. Make this your top priority in life and let everything else be subservient to this.

CHAPTER 5

ORDER OUT OF CHAOS

It's not uncommon to feel as though the world is caving in on you. The world can be an unfriendly and sinister place. Life gets chaotic sometimes. But amid chaos there's always order, the divine order for your life. I would like to compare getting order out of chaos to confusion in a courtroom: everyone is gathered in one place to defend and argue their cases in hopes of winning and being acquitted.

In the courtroom you'll find the plaintiff, defendant, witnesses, spectators, law enforcement officers, court stenographer, jury, attorneys, and judge. Then suddenly, there's a volcanic eruption of built-up hatred, anger, and frustration that breaks out and the courtroom is filled with chaos. There's yelling, swearing, and even fighting going on. Immediately, the judge picks up his or her gavel, strikes it against a sounding block (to bring down the gavel means to compel or enforce with the authority of the court), and then the judge speaks five words that the entire U.S. judicial system supports: "ORDER! ORDER IN THE COURT!" Five authoritative words instantly released restraining power and control, and within minutes everything went back to order and the original purpose for that trial, and those who were held in contempt of court were arrested and removed from the courtroom.

Our storms in life are like that courtroom, and there are times when we need God, the Righteous Judge, to intervene by swiftly speaking "ORDER!" back into the courtrooms of our lives. "Then He arose and rebuked the wind, and said unto the sea, 'Peace, be still!' And the wind ceased and there was a great calm" (Mark 4:39).

However, when His voice is silent, we must know

that He's given us the same authority to speak *order* into our own lives by using His Word. All of Heaven's judicial system is backing the authoritative Word when spoken. That's right! Every chaotic situation (storm) in our lives must subside when this occurs. "For God is not the author of confusion but of peace..." (I Corinthians 14:33).

In other words, when confusion breaks out in your home, on your job, or in your business or ministry and when bad things happen to you and your loved ones — like in the comparison of the courtroom — you've been given the spiritual *judicial* authority to end the confusion by *speaking authoritatively to those storms.* Now mind you, the power's not in your tone of voice, but in His choice of Words and mighty name! And even if you don't see results right away, continue to speak until the job is done! In turn, your disorderly circumstances in life will then go back to normalcy.

But bear in mind that the wills of other people are involved in your conflict, and no one — including God — can control the will of another person unless they yield to His order, or unless they are under the control of some form of witchcraft, etc. Disruptions in life that turn into chaos are nothing more than setbacks that are orchestrated to ambush your goals and wreak havoc on the good success of your future. No one can deny that life is difficult sometimes, but anything worthwhile is difficult.

Life and Its Purpose

The most important thing about this life is learning how to live it. To understand life's purpose, one must know the meaning of life. And the true meaning of life is *freedom.* We are born free. However, freedom can be interpreted in many different ways by many different people. Freedom is really all about being unrestricted to fulfill your purpose in life without being controlled by necessity or fate.

Nothing is more rewarding than understanding what you were born to do and then being free to successfully do it. Everything in life begins with a solid foundation of freedom on which we are to build, along with the blueprints of the original plan and purpose. To deviate from this foundation means to invite the circumstances in life that enslave, causing hurt and pain.

The way you build your life from this pivotal point determines whether or not you will experience bondage or true liberty throughout the rest of your life. Chaotic bondage, on the other hand, is the binding force that hinders the good things you desire to do, and it's the prevention of what you desire to have in life.

Consider what takes place when the original plan is disrupted: a motor vehicle was originally designed to provide safe transportation for us. But when an accident occurs, causing both severe injury to an individual and damage to the vehicle, it alters the original purpose for that vehicle. And albeit it was designed with safety mechanisms, such as an air bag, etc., precious lives still sometimes end in tragic deaths.

This is a vivid image and definition of the chaos of life. So now the question is, how do we get order out of chaos, especially chaos of this magnitude? It's accomplished by remembering to do what the judge did in his courtroom, and then reiterate. Moreover, accomplishing this task requires taking one step backward to remember your plan and purpose, because in the heat of the battle of confusion, you sometimes forget. (Your purpose is the contrast of your trial.) And then prepare to take with you only that which is salvageable from your injuries and damages in life, while leaving the rest behind; and finally, you advance forward with a vision-driven victor's determination to try, once again, to reach that finish line!

Let me give you another illustration: when a train has been derailed but the scheduled plan is to keep moving forward, the engineer of that train must stop and recall the original plan. Then he or she has to implement *order* (change) by focusing on getting the train back on course. Otherwise, the train will be hindered from getting to its destination on time, and the derailment will lead it elsewhere. Once the train is back on track, it will move full speed ahead.

When your life is temporarily derailed, for whatever

reason and for whatever season, just remember where you're headed and what you set out to do, and then continue doing it. And above all else, keep your frame of reference and get to where you're going.

When *good* is the final destination of the circumstances of life, *evil* will always be present to try to derail the trip. But just as you didn't quit before, I'm sure that you won't quit now. Your determination to win sharpens your edge and gives you heads-up on a victorious outcome.

Getting order out of chaos may seem impossible when trials come all at one time and from every direction—or perhaps they come repeatedly, one after another—but know this: your purpose has promising power, and it will stay the course, and it's only a matter of time before that promise purpose is fulfilled. In due time, you will understand *life and its purpose.* So allow the virtue of patience to complete its work and course. Your season of peace in chaotic times and your vision of living a better life are expeditiously approaching.

New Life After Divorce

It is common knowledge that the current divorce rate is at an all-time high of nearly fifty percent in America. A marriage can be dissolved on-line these days and executed within a short period of time. It behooves you to know that breaking the covenant of marriage has become an epidemic in our society. It seems as though only a small amount of people view marriage as an actual covenant. Perhaps most see it as an arrangement of superficial convenience with the conditions being, *give me what I need and want, when I need and want it, or it's over and I'm out of here!*

Clearly, there are some biblical grounds for divorce that I will not hesitate to mention, such as desertion, adultery, and life-threatening abuse. But even these sins can be forgiven. However, when I talk to hurting people, before and after their divorce, I seldom hear of the biblical reasons for why they were divorced or desire to be divorced. Perhaps the real problem comes in three forms: (1) There is a lack of reverential fear of

God and what He hates (Malachi 2:16). (2) People rush and marry total strangers and later find themselves spiritually, sexually, intellectually, and even financially unequally yoked. (3) Lust is oftentimes mistaken for love. If you are the victim of—and desire to become the victor over—divorce, then this word of exhortation is for your heart: you will never find total contentment with another person and you will never experience a greater love than the love of God. We cannot receive from others what they are incapable of giving.

Divorce was inevitable for those who were broken from the beginning, because when broken people are not fixed and healed, dissolution of marriage is always the outcome unless God is allowed to intervene. Divorce, for some people, can be like a sudden death, only worse. With death you receive closure after a while, but with a divorce that involves children, you're made to feel forever connected to the pain of it all. But just because you feel that way doesn't mean that you're still connected. You're not just free, but free indeed. And when you stop and think about it, we really don't walk by feelings, do we?

"We walk by faith!" And faith always believes that "God causes everything to work together for the good of those who love God and are called according to his purpose for them" (Romans 8:28).

This means, in essence, that God's ultimate plan will prevail in your life and family. And at this present time it may look like you've received the bad end of the stick (you can't pay your accumulated debt, you don't know who to trust, and you're feeling alone, hurt, confused, angry, etc.), while others continue to "prosper" and get away with murder—so to speak—and it may look as though you're the only culprit. Moreover, your heart may still be breaking because you now have a broken home. But there's *one thing I've learned about life: it always demands a retrial!* And this new trial is granted upon the motion of the *losing party,* based on newly-discovered evidence, or obvious error.

Additionally, whatever injustice is inflicted upon another individual is guaranteed to return to the sender. Becoming a whole person again is what's needed now. However, the remedy for being whole again, to some people, is to immediately re-marry someone else while they're still crushed and deeply wounded inside. But, be advised, re-marriage without grounds for divorce and before the appointed time could be detrimental, causing history to repeat itself in one way or another. Victims of divorce will need time, much time, to heal in order to prevent inflicting their repressed pain on the innocent new person—and believe me, the time will come when the new relationships will remind them of their painful past. All it will take is for someone to push the right buttons and "Cruella de Ville" or the "Incredible Hulk" (fictional characters) will appear. They will also need time to discern what the new person in their life may be hiding from them.

Dishonesty is always a by-product of all superficial people until they get what they want, and then you discover their true motives for being in your life. Try your best not to rush this crucial time and part of your life, because *becoming whole again takes time.* Be willing to admit that you *broke a covenant* that was witnessed by God, whether it was a Christian or non-Christian wedding. Truly repent of having done it, forgive and release the other person, receive God's forgiveness and then move on!

Make it your business to find out who you really are now and what you have to offer another person before you marry again. Purpose in your heart to give someone your very best, just as you deserve. Learn how to be content with your current life while you're planning for a better one. This will prevent you from rushing in and failing again. And whatever you do, don't engage yourself with anyone on the rebound; it will only bring guaranteed disaster.

Be sure to place compatibility—especially spiritual—above attraction, because being attracted to someone doesn't necessarily mean that person is right for you. Go ahead and dream big this time! It's okay to do so. But also use wisdom! Imagine yourself having a life of love, joy, peace, and prosperity with someone who loves and serves God and who will love and cherish you.

Or, for others of you, your dream may be to never commit to anyone again. Whichever the case, learn to love "you" for a change while you wait for your true purpose vision to come to pass. Learning to love and feel good about yourself will release all the hostility associated with abuse, abandonment, infidelity, etc., and it will free you from that mental and emotional prison of blaming yourself for it all.

The healing of your wounded heart is very essential now. And I reiterate: if you don't allow ample time for healing, you will unconsciously experience spasmodic emotional outbursts that will make those around you quite miserable, while they confusedly try to love you. Additionally, reinvent yourself while in your holding place. Do what you never took time to do before, such as:

- Lose weight
- Learn a new sport
- Get your first degree or another one
- Apply for a promotion in your job
- Join the singles' group at your church
- Start your own business
- Relocate to a new city

- Apply for a new job

- Befriend someone

- Travel to another country

- Take a vacation to an exotic island (now, this one I'm ready for!)

Actively engaging yourself in one or more of these things will temporarily take the place of "much-needed" companionship, and this should sustain you until you're ripe and ready—through and through—for that true love that never fails. And while reinventing (transforming) the physical and soulish part of you, remember to renew your spirit and reach for a higher spiritual goal. "Forgetting those things which are behind and reaching forward to those things which are ahead, I press toward the goal for the prize…" (Philippians 3:13, 14).

I am a firm believer that people enter our lives for two reasons: to *hinder* or to enhance. If the person you married did nothing but hinder you or cause you harm, you can choose to grow from that painful experience and become a better person. Or, if they tried to *enhance* you and succeeded to a degree, then mature from that vantage point, as well. Perhaps you were that diamond in the rough that needed the laser drilling to burn out the black carbon inclusions in your character, and that fifty-eight-faceted cut to make your life brilliantly beautiful and count for something.

Unequivocally, there is another life after divorce for those who lay hold of God's unmerited mercy and grace. It's unmerited because the penalty for what was done (which was the thing that He hates) should have been much more severe than what was experienced. God's grace and favor opens new doors to life after the closing of others, and in return, He expects pure gratitude for His kindness to you and ungrudging forgiveness to those who have wronged you.

When you're ready to begin anew, you must first rise up out of that horrible pit that divorce put you in and allow God to restore your soul which consists of your mind, will, and emotions. Receive healing for your *mind* to dispel your old dysfunctional way of thinking; and the yielding of your *will*, which is bound to be set on doing things your way now; and the healing of your *emotions*, which fluctuate like the weather.

Determine not to carry any of the heavy baggage from your past experiences into your future, neither failures nor successes. Now, what do I mean by this? Failure, obviously, causes hurt to resurface itself, but beware of successes as well, because dwelling on successes can sometimes cause you to compare what you had or did before to what you have and are doing now. However, by doing this, you run the risk of intimidating and/or rejecting someone that you feel doesn't measure up; consequently, this will adversely affect them and could possibly drive them away.

While establishing new relationships and building your bridge of forgiveness, remember to exercise the power of *forgetfulness* as well, and then you'll begin to understand and appreciate the power of renewed love and its healing remedies. Be knowledgeable of the fact that wounded people hurt other people; however I do think it's cowardice for people who inflict pain to use this statement as an excuse to do so. This is important because it happens all the time. Become that big little person who executes your right of refusal to not *punish* another individual simply because you were punished.

Build a support team by acquainting yourself with people who edify and support you, and cherish those who invest in your success and your future. Identify and remove all toxic people from your life because toxins kill and destroy. Again, it's okay. There are plenty of new people who will celebrate you and not just tolerate you. See the past failures as a boot camp that made you fit for the beauty of what is to come. You can't erase the past, but you can establish a new future—one day at a time.

A senior pastor, who lived in California with his lovely wife and two small children, experienced life's best and literally had it all. This pastor was a great orator who was well-known for his powerful messages that denounced divorce. People from his fellowship expressed different opinions about his messages. Some said the messages were very life-changing, others said they were judgmental and condemning and only placed emphasis on "how much God hates divorce," and on how "true Christians should know better, because it's a sin!" Thousands of people would gather on Sundays to hear words of hope, but instead they heard these words and left hurt and disappointed. As the church grew, the demand to pastor so many people became overwhelming. He spent countless hours counseling the married couples as well as the single adults.

The pastor's rule of thumb was to not counsel singles without his mate or one of his associate ministers being present. However, on this one occasion, the pastor let his guard down and made an exception. Through his office door walked a stunningly beautiful new church member, with whom he was not acquainted. This woman absolutely took his breath away! While enraptured by her beauty, he was completely lost for words. Minutes later he managed to say to her, "Please, have a seat." As she poured out her heart to him, he began to relate to some of her problems, and said, "I do understand, I've been there." Then suddenly, he realized that they both had a lot in common. And although he had concealed his true feelings of dissatisfaction, of boredom, and of being sexually neglected in his own marriage, he found himself opening up to her. In a very short period of time, their pastor/parishioner relationship turned into an adulterous affair.

When his wife and congregation found out about it, he denied it, of course, for fear of losing everything. Later on, the truth was revealed by the woman in the affair. In fact, she told his wife that she was only there for that reason, because she hated pastors due to her painful past experiences with them. *"Beware of wolves in sheep's clothing!"*

Sadly enough, the marriage of this prominent leader ended in divorce, and the man who had preached to so many people that "God hates divorce" was now experiencing the same pain himself. "If another believer is overcome by some sin, you who are godly should gently and humbly help that person back onto the right path. *And be careful not to fall into the same temptation yourself"* (Galatians 6:1).

I know it's very hard to practice what you preach; however, it's absolutely necessary for us to exercise meekness when correcting others who miss the mark. (A great lesson for *us* to learn.) Amid all of his personal pain, the pastor fervently repented and asked God, his wife, and his congregation for forgiveness. But to his wife, infidelity was grounds for divorce. And so reconciliation was completely out of the question. She wanted out, because her heart had been hardened and deeply crushed by this. She vowed never to trust or love a man like that again, especially pastors and men in the church. Obviously, she stopped believing that marriage is made up of two forgivers and forgetters of the wrong that was done. "If you forgive those who sin against you, your heavenly Father will forgive you. But if you refuse to forgive others, your Father will not forgive your sins" (Matthew 6:14, 15).

Later that year, the pastor was totally restored and well received by his congregation. A few years later he met and married a professional woman in corporate America, who had been single for many years with two children of her own. Together they became a family of six: the pastor, his wife, and their four children. They grew together in harmony and in the love of God and became the ideal family as leaders in their community, primarily because of their mutual love and respect for one another, and also because they didn't exclude the birth parents of their children, nor did they implement hatred toward them, which can be very damaging to children. Unlike most families of divorce, they all were mature enough to come together as often as they could, if for nothing else but to ensure the emotional stability and spiritual welfare of their precious children.

God, in His loving kindness and tender mercies, forgave the pastor; the pastor forgave his former wife for leaving him; the former wife found the grace to forgive the pastor; the new wife forgave the father of her children; and thus the healing power of forgiveness, love, and acceptance began and continued throughout their marriage, family, and ministry.

This is a vivid picture of what God's infinite love looks like. God's amazing grace is for everyone, but not many pastors have made this kind of comeback. The alarming truth is that a large number of pastors *quit* after a crash of this magnitude. But on the other hand, far too many continue without being reprimanded and without repenting. And some continue with business as usual without allowing an allotted time for healing to take place.

Quite clearly, this family would not have become a testimony of God's mercy and amazing grace had the minds of this leader and his family been viciously poisoned against the other people involved. What kind of spiritual leader and his wife (often the real hidden assassin) would turn the hearts of their innocent children against their own birth parents, especially if they are not abusive and unfit? Surely, this is not how true love operates. Thankfully, there are wonderful step-parents who truly love *all* of their step-children as their own. This fallen pastor, who was loved and disliked by so many people, received a second chance and found *new life after divorce.*

Starving For Intimacy

I'm sure you realize that separations and divorces don't just happen overnight. Something serious must have played an integral part in the break-up. Could one of the reasons be the lack of romantic or passionate sexual activity? Intimacy plays an important role in the human experience of every relationship. Humans are created with a desire to love and be loved by someone, which is usually satisfied through sexual intercourse.

Strong emotional attachments are formed when two people merge their affections for one another sexually, a bond that's so magnificent that it has the power to create another human being. Amazing! Utterly amazing! Intimacy is such an awesome gift from God, but sadly, it's been perverted and abused by so many.

Think for a moment: when God created the woman for the man, He blessed their union with sexual intimacy. "Then God looked over all He had made, and He saw that it was very good" (Genesis 1:31)! This included sexual intimacy, which was required in order for them to reproduce, "be fruitful and multiply." The very act itself was viewed as "very good"—so good, in fact, that even in this day and age, *the last orgasm commands a standing ovation and an "encore," over and over again!* I'm sure you're smiling right now, but don't smile too much because someone might see you and wonder why you're enjoying this part of the book. Once a bond is created through sexual intimacy, the body adapts to what it was created for: "Now Adam had sexual relations with his wife, Eve, and she became pregnant..." (Genesis 4:1).

But here's the part that's so interesting: the body goes into shock when deprived of sexual intimacy. It's kind of like going on an absolute fast with no food, only water for a long period of time. The body begins to pull from its resources and stores fat when it thinks it's being starved. And so it is with the body and intimacy: a person feels starved and begins to look for fulfillment in all the wrong places, including the Internet.

Sexual intimacy is so powerfully connected to the mind that when a person—depraved in their thinking— goes without it, they can be tempted to forcibly take it from another person—any person, including children, or they gaze upon it through pornography.

It troubles my heart to say that pornography is the number one stronghold in the lives of many Christians today. This is the debauched version of sexual intimacy! Marriage covenants are broken all the time, because a marriage partner can never compete with the characters and their conduct in pornography.

It's really not a good thing to be in a marriage and withhold yourself (sexual intercourse) from your mate, except for physical reasons, and prayer and fasting. "The husband should fulfill his wife's sexual needs, and the wife should fulfill her husband's needs. *Do not deprive each other of sexual relations,* unless you both agree to refrain from sexual intimacy for a limited time so you can give yourselves more completely to prayer. Afterward, you should come together so that Satan won't be able to tempt you because of your lack of self-control" (I Corinthians 7:3, 5).

Husbands and their wives are often tempted when this occurs, and some find themselves yielding to the temptation. *The infidelity of a mate may be an indication that a mate's changing sexual desires are no longer being satisfied within their marriage covenant.* They frequently have sex, but they complain of not having good sex. Serious problems will often surface from disparity of sex drives between two people. It seems that some people are wired for sexual intimacy and they hop from person to person and carry on like little rabbits, while others can simply do without. If these two opposites attract, there will be grave repercussions. Whenever there's a loss or lack of sexual desire in a mate, this places a strain on the relationship, which is often displayed through frustration, hostility, loneliness, depression, isolation, etc.

Sexual Appetites

Sexuality varies, depending on the individual. There are distinct differences between the male and female sex drives. Getting a clear understanding of this truth before you marry could save you from embarrassment, heartache, and even despair. Gaining knowledge will also help bring clarity to the confusion associated with a man's racy, persistent sexual appetite and a woman's withdrawn, declining sexual appetite, or vice versa.

The Female Sex Drive

When it comes to fully comprehending the structural maze of a woman and the female orgasm, most men are totally confused about how it all works. If you study anatomy, which is a great way to prepare for your future or present mate, you'll discover that the makeup of a woman is that of a receiver, and the makeup of a man is that of a giver.

When desiring to please a woman (marriage partner), consider the fact that most women have intercourse regularly, but very few experience the joys of orgasmic pleasure, which they should experience time and time again, and well into their nineties. Why is this true? Well, I'll try to elaborate on it discreetly. It is often the result of a woman not positioning herself correctly for the trigger points of her body to be effected (so men, you're not always to blame). Or perhaps it's due to her mate rushing ahead of her to the finish line. Achieving satisfaction in sexual intimacy is fifty percent what you do, and fifty percent what he does. If you don't know your own body and what you desire, your mate will not know, either. (The two of you should experiment.)

However, you are actually the one in control of your sexual appetite and desires being fulfilled during sexual intimacy. You can't wait for someone else to do all the work for you. So, instead of being the receiver all the time, you'll have to become the giver/receiver. Choosing the right position puts you in control of when and how you reach your sexual euphoria.

With this in mind, it is important to *get in shape and stay in shape* so that you'll have the confidence you need to *take charge,* as well as be pleasing for him to gaze upon. Additionally, your emotions should be totally involved in the act of lovemaking, and your mind should not be elsewhere. To fully enjoy your time of sexual intimacy, you *must* temporarily block out *all* your distractions, all your duties, and focus on him alone. Setting the mood actually sets the tone for what can occur. If your man is a giver/forerunner, he will take pleasure in considering you *first*. (There now, was that discreet enough for you?) Okay, great; now let's continue.

Too often married couples become frustrated with one another because their feelings of disappointment are not communicated or understood. And then, after a short period of time, the woman *fakes it until she makes it*. However, this unpleasant state can be avoided when you both do your part. Obviously, what this means is that you must be mentally and emotionally prepared to receive and then give your all, and he must be willing to give his all and then receive, and vice versa.

In the beginning, the man should try to hold on long enough to incorporate the foreplay that relaxes and stimulates every part of his mate, as well as allow the levels of her *estrogen* (sex hormone) to increase. After all, the man is the giver and the initiator in this area, right? *Anyone can have sex, but the gift of lovemaking is an art.* Once this mission is accomplished, he's either half-way there or has hit the target! At this point, the trumpets should be sounding, the banners should be waving and the band should be playing! Upon completion, they both should be *singing their favorite songs!*

The Male Sex Drive

Men and women are not only diverse in their body structure, but also perceptually and mentally regarding sexual intimacy as well. It is true that both men and women tend to fantasize about sexual intimacy, but it is believed that men fantasize more often, and actually desire sexual intimacy more than women. Perhaps this helps to explain why men can sometimes have a heated discussion with their mates one minute, and then be ready for an *Oscar-winning performance* in the bedroom, or right where you are, the next minute. Fantasizing about sexual intimacy is one thing, but acting out that fantasy is another thing.

Often a man envisions what he desires, and when the opportunity presents itself, he becomes motivated by what he sees, and then carries out his plan. This is what determines the real difference between male and female sex drives. Men will be up for it whether you are or not. (Remember this when the headaches come and your emotions are completely out of balance due to life's demands and disappointments.)

The *turbo* sex drive of most men enables them to accomplish their goals during sexual intimacy, and then they gladly move on with their day. However, penetration means absolutely nothing to some women, if the sexual intimacy doesn't begin with the involvement of her emotions. Most women want to be enraptured by love (fully enveloped), covered with your love, and not just entered by your love. And if the women are honest, they will concur that when they are *not* there emotionally in the act of lovemaking, they're not there physically. She may be there in your arms for the moment, but mentally she's also preparing dinner, doing the laundry, caring for the children, checking her email, shopping, or perhaps taking a romantic trip to Paris.

In order for her to be in-to you, you'll have to be in-to her. This should begin days, weeks, and even months in advance, leading up to lovemaking. Here's the beauty of it all: we were not created to have the same sex drives.

Being different always enhances the competitiveness. So, remember to celebrate who you are, and appreciate who they are, and then discover what could happen when opposites attract.

Your desire to please your mate will result in your mate desiring to please you, and this is no doubt what sexual intimacy is all about. (Think of how beautiful and exploratory sexual intimacy can be!) Mutual respect is also a key factor in experiencing climactic pleasure. No one gives themselves to another person when there's disrespect. If a woman has lost respect for you, her highly esteeming you and being passionate with you will also be lost. If this is one of the reasons for the decrease in her sex drive, and you still desire her intimately, then find out what the problem is with you, and try to fix it. Sometimes all the counseling in the world will not suffice until the changes in what she believes to be *annoying habits or character flaws* take place in you.

In addition, to receive her respect, you must win her friendship and trust. If you have wronged her in any way, sincerely ask her for forgiveness, and guard against making the same mistakes again. Ease her mind of the possibility of infidelity. Cherish her, and adore her body as it is now, and then praise her when and if she's able to perfect it. And try not to ever disregard her in any way. Once simple alterations such as these are made, and more, your refrigerated bedroom will become a hothouse, in some cases.

Ultimately, your highly increased *testosterone* levels (sex hormone) will thank you, and you'll have more functioning power. Instead of finding an excuse to stay away from her or from home all the time, you'll enjoy the pleasures of entering your castle and being greeted like a king. She may even become your new *wife* and your *mistress*, who fulfills all of your needs.

The Sexual Language of Love

In addition, poor communication between marriage partners regarding their sexual preferences and needs are also important factors in breakups. When the language of love is absent from sexual intimacy, it weakens the pleasure. But when *decent* sounds of love are expressed, it heightens the euphoric experience.

Communication between you and your mate during sexual intimacy eliminates the curiosity of whether or not pleasure is being achieved, and allows you to focus on your main goal. It also breaks the silence when you're both feeling awkward while experimenting and enjoying love. Remember, your words are extremely powerful, and they play an integral part in the anticipated outcome of the act of sexual intimacy.

Single and Sexually Satisfied

Now, what I'm about to reveal next is going to seem impossible for many of you, but here goes: it would be wise for you as a single person to withhold sexual intimacy until married to prevent forming an attachment with someone that's not meant for you. Caution! Sexual soul ties (bonds) are hard to break! And when you do meet the right person, the new relationship will be crowded with a third person. This is clinically proven.

The powerful hormone called oxytocin serves as a neurotransmitter in the brain and plays a big role in emotional bonding. It is often referred to as the "love molecule" or "trust hormone." The brain releases low levels of oxytocin whenever there's bodily contact. This hormone is also greatly stimulated during sexual intimacy; the more sex, the greater the bond. This should give you a better understanding of why some people "fall in love" so easily and find it difficult to release someone, even after the relationship ends.

Most people tend to be enamored with an instant attraction or bonding, both in romantic encounters and friendships. And we all tend to believe that bonding (developing closeness) with someone quickly is a sure sign of a compatible connection, a kindred spirit, etc. How many times have you heard people say, "The moment we met, we hit it off right away," or "Immediately I was swept off my feet"? Realistically speaking, *instant compatible romances* rarely turn out to be as lasting as they initially seem. Often they are warning signs of imminent danger, which will eventually lead to someone being seriously hurt. And ultimately, for some relationships, the instant romances simply fade away.

Don't misunderstand me; there are some marriages that end in divorce due to sexual incompatibility, even though they proceeded this way with caution. However, if you trust God and ask for His wisdom regarding this matter, He will guide you when choosing a mate.

The Benefits of Sexual Intimacy

I find that a lot has been said to condemn adultery, and rightfully so—but there's not enough said about withholding sexual intimacy from a marriage partner for selfish reasons and about fornication. Consequently, *in some cases*, there are two hurting people involved in infidelity: the husband and the wife. One withheld their sexual intimacy and the other one released it—to someone else. But amid these dark clouds of selfishness and unfaithfulness, there still remain at least eleven benefits of sexual intimacy that go untapped:

- It releases stress

- It enhances sleep

- It can cure headaches

- It increases blood flow

- It increases the heart rate and brain power

- It burns up to one thousand calories

- It creates new life (conception and childbirth)

- It guards against infidelity

- It renews youthfulness

- It affirms self-worth

- It creates oneness

If you've ever said, "I love you" to someone and meant it, then surely you can rekindle that love and mean it now, because true love never fails. Love is more than something you say; it's what you do! *Lovemaking,* versus having sex, is the expression of the love you feel for each other; *it's also creating love that's tailored to fit the sexual desires of the one you truly love.* (Each encounter should be an adventure, from foreplay to climax!) Now, if you both feel this way, then the intimacy will indeed be satisfying and explosive!

Relationships that last are the ones that give and keep on giving, forgive and keep on forgiving, and love and keep on loving one another. Genesis 2:18 says, "It is not good for the man to be alone. I will make a helper who is just right for him." Therefore, no one should be without love and companionship, unless they choose to be; and no marriage should be without the gift of love and sexual intimacy.

It doesn't matter the amount of damage that was done to you as a single or married person that warrants throwing in the towel and calling it quits, you can get *order out of chaos.* And you can end the incessant cycle of sexual deprivation in your marriage by letting go of the past hurt and distrust (however, this process of letting go may require Christian counseling) and also by lovingly redirecting your wounded heart, that's *starving for intimacy,* to its original connection, and then pray that your love will eventually be received.

CHAPTER 6

EXTRACTING THE GOOD

A re you familiar with the process of extracting? To extract means to remove something by pressure, such as using our kitchen tool: the power juicer. More than anything else that's involved in the process, pressure is the most required to extricate juice from fruits and vegetables. And the same applies to extracting the good out of life—with all of its pain and sorrows, and gloomy outlooks for our tomorrows, you must apply and allow pressure. It's time for the extracting of the good to begin, which means two things: you must desire good things to happen to you and you must understand the purpose for life's pressures.

Whenever you find yourself under a tremendous amount of pressure, remember this: you can't get extra virgin olive oil from a ripe olive without it being hard pressed. And as strange as it may seem, this is God's way of removing all that is a deterrent in your life, while bringing forth that which is priceless in you.

Two five-year-old, audacious twin brothers were well-known for their karate and wrestling abilities. They constantly challenged one another and sought the performance appraisal of their dad, who was a body builder.

After working out with their dad they looked forward to the special beverages that their mom prepared for them, and so they would run to the kitchen and watch their mom use her juicer. They witnessed their fruits and veggies going in one way and coming out another. One day, while their mother was resting, the first twin decided to teach his brother a lesson, so he grabbed the juicer from the counter and tried to force his brother's head into the container. The mom heard the second twin shouting for help and ran into the kitchen. She shouted, "What are you doing?!" And the culprit said, "He keeps on bothering me and he needs to change. So I'm putting him in your machine!" Children will be children.

Don't throw away ten, maybe twenty years of your life because of failures. And don't conceal traumatic experiences that almost destroyed your life, because concealment confines you. But boldly come forth with the truth and extract every good life lesson that was learned from those negative experiences and circumstances, even though this form of extraction (pressure) may be painful. And then continue to extract regularly.

It's Not the End

The fact that you made it to this part of this chapter is proof that it's not the end, but a means to new beginnings from the end of your hopeless situations. This includes financial ruin such as: *a foreclosure, a bankruptcy, a failed business venture, a bad investment, or accumulated debt.* If you've experienced any of the above setbacks, know that you're not alone in this world. You're actually in good company. Having experienced financial ruin says something about you, and that is: *at least you tried!* You took a risk, and risk is what life's all about. Without taking the risk you never would have known whether or not you could have succeeded. This is why when people grow older they speak more of what they regret not doing than what they did do. The only thing that's certain about life is death; *so you must keep trying to succeed* and enjoy the journey while you can.

The funny thing about life is that it has a way of coming full circle if allowed to run its course. If you've not advanced in what you were born to do, and have not circulated back to the starting point of your journey of life, then you haven't reached the end. You may have reached the end of your rope, due to these setbacks, but not the end of your season of life. If the majority of your time has been spent anxiously worrying about your financial difficulties, then you haven't really lived your life yet.

Full circle is a 360-degree turn—not a 180-degree

turn. There's still time left for you to turn things around in your life, no matter what mistakes you've made. Learn the proper way to process the pain of failure. Change the way you manage your money and the way you conduct business in the future. Now that you've picked yourself up by your bootstraps and dusted yourself off, try not to do anything else until you seek expert advice this time around. And when wisdom speaks, you need to listen in order to learn. Let's examine the above list of setbacks:

Foreclosure

If you have experienced a foreclosure, then you know the devastating affect this can have on a person and their family. The damage to your credit is enough to make you want to find a cave and move into it, not to mention the embarrassment associated with it. Let's look at ways to get something good out of this bad situation:

The Extract:

Foreclosure is proof that people live beyond their

means, sometimes their income is less than their monthly expenditures, or in some cases, it's the result of a loss of some sort, or emergencies which became top priorities, and then consequently, the mortgage went unpaid. But I have good news: this locates you and reveals the need for more knowledge regarding money management. And like anything else, stewardship requires training.

You can bounce back and repair your credit with the help of professionals in this field. And as for the embarrassment associated with all foreclosures, don't allow yourself to be embarrassed, because you are not alone. Millions of Americans have been there; so when applying for a rental home or an apartment, trust that the decision makers will consider this when they run your credit.

You can start over with new wise choices now, because the burden of possessing too much, having extravagant taste without extravagant money, or perhaps trying to impress people with material things to be accepted has been lifted. This devastating outcome will test the love and friendship of family and friends. Some people will desert those they say they love in troubled times like these. Better to find out now than to be forever deceived by their hypocrisy.

Bankruptcy

I truly believe that everyone has experienced some form of bankruptcy in their lives, whether it's mental, emotional, spiritual, physical, or financial. To be bankrupt is to be legally declared unable to pay debts; it leaves a person drained, lacking, or deficient. Bankruptcy leads to the place of no return, which ultimately is a state of ruin, or poverty. It's much more severe than the inability to pay a mortgage; it's failure on a wide scale.

In our society, filing for bankruptcy says a lot about an individual. It labels people before they have a chance to recover and prove themselves otherwise, and creditors stereotype them before they even get the chance to meet them. On paper they are declared a failure. For some people, bankruptcy simply becomes a way of escape from all their financial obligations. However, in God's eyes bankruptcy does not define you, nor does it reflect how He sees you. You are not a failure to Him, because He created you in His image and likeness.

What God sees is the wrong paths that we often take and the wrong choices that we sometimes make, trying to find our way in this world, and although wrong paths and wrong choices are a sure recipe for disaster, He's always there to pick us up when we fall and to answer when we call.

The Extract:

To be bankrupt financially is indeed the same as being bankrupt emotionally and spiritually. The three are in many ways connected. When it's emotional and spiritual, it's generally the result of hardships that take a toll on a person, which in turn affects their ability to succeed or make a living. When life has no meaning, this is the outcome. But there's good that can come out of bankruptcy once your mind-set regarding it changes.

When people are in need of something and they are unable to pay cash for it, they look to creditors for help. With excitement they take possession of something that doesn't belong to them, but to the creditors. However, when payments are missed, the creditors take back what they own. Fulfilling an obligation should be done with gratitude, not grudgingly. In this case, we see selfishness and ungratefulness and a need for change—a need to grow up.

Contact your creditors to give an explanation for the bankruptcy: a death in the family, an illness, etc. When forced to file for bankruptcy, be thankful for the cancellation of your debt, but know that this form of cancellation (bankruptcy) is not His best. And then decide not to travel this road ever again.

A Failed Business Venture

You invest in a business in hopes of succeeding and becoming financially secure. You work hard, long hours. You sacrifice everything and barely make ends meet. Right? Then one day the report comes across your desk that says your business is operating in the red. So you search for answers and ways to rise above it, to no avail. Failing in business is not the end of you achieving great success one day. But it does speak of the failure to carry out a plan and to reach a goal. It also reveals the absence of strong leadership and the inability to properly delegate to others, and perhaps the mishandling of funds.

Even your location may have played a part in the failure. And the list goes on and on. Sometimes the wrong motive for starting a business can play a key part in a failing business venture: for example, if you dream a dream that belongs to someone else and then try to carry it out, you'll fail; if you begin your venture trying to impress people with your knowledge apart from wisdom and experience, you'll fail miserably; and if you don't fully understand the concept of business, which basically is providing a service—*the best possible service*—to meet the needs of others, you'll quit.

The Extract:

Opportunities knock quite frequently in America. Those who fail in one business venture can recover and try again, or build a new business altogether. If there was any amount of financial success, then you achieved what others only dreamed of doing. At least you tried to do something with a golden opportunity. If building again is not in your plan, then glean from the wisdom of your success and failure and begin mentoring others.

After all the mistakes that were made, I'm sure you've learned wise life lessons on trust, loyalty, and dedication as you witnessed the lack of it in your own organization. Now you have clearly discovered what it really takes to open and operate a business and to succeed at doing it. Being in business for yourself means providing a "high in demand" service of some sort, which differs from your competition, to your community and beyond.

Perhaps now, after experiencing some minor or major setbacks, you understand the importance of hiring the right staff and providing the best customer service, with satisfaction guaranteed. These things can make or break a successful business, as can having integrity and using wise money management skills.

Bad Investments

Now, we all should know that everything that looks

like gold is not always gold. You may have been quite sure that this new venture would be the investment that would yield great dividends. Thousands of dollars are invested in projects all the time. Wall Street is full of opportunists. But not every potential gold mine investment that people make is made with wisdom and sound judgment. Some people invest out of what they call "luck or chance."

When operating by luck a person makes room for the option of bad fortune to happen as well as good. Good fortune, on the other hand, is success due to chance. Much study and research should precede whimsical investments, especially if investing in someone else's business or project. Investing your money in the wrong projects is like playing the lottery: a lot of money in for someone else to win, but nothing in return for you. Remember, fast money is just that: FAST MONEY! Easy come, easy go! However, doing the right things in life in terms of acquiring and managing money requires knowledge and patience. A get-rich-quick mentality only leads to poverty. (Read Proverbs 28:22 NLT.)

The Extract:

If you have invested in projects that yielded no return, and now, so much money has been lost, don't dwell on the loss, but grasp the concept of sowing and reaping and then implement it. And expect a harvest one day on what you've sown into good ground this time around. Trust me, your harvest will be the result of the Law of Reciprocity at work (what you sow, you will reap). Bad investments are like bad seeds sown into bad soil that produces no harvest. But seeds that are sown into good ground produce after their kind.

To prevent this from ever happening again, it would be wise to only invest in what has been proven (tried, tested, and well established) to yield rich dividends, like the work of ministry, outreaches that feed the poor, etc. And due to a failing economy, it would be wise not to invest in some projects at all in such turbulent times. Understand that money takes wings and flies, and is very uncertain. It can be here in your possession one day, and gone the next. With knowledge of this truth, you should use extreme caution and invest your hard earned money more wisely in the future.

Let me offer a word of encouragement: if you were chosen to handle wealth once, you may very well be chosen to manage it again. Not everyone can be trusted with the title *financier*. You have what it takes or you would not have made it this far. The money would not have been there to invest in the first place, if it was not appointed for you to do so.

Debt Accumulation

Debt accumulation is obviously the culmination of neglect and lack. If you had it within your means to pay your debts but didn't, this is called neglect. If you had money and spent it on something else, this is called being irresponsible. And if you experienced the loss of a job and had difficulties finding another one, or if you have no savings or any other source of income to pay your bills, this is called lack.

However, life does have a way of throwing curve balls that catch you off guard sometimes. That's why preparedness is paramount. Having something to fall back on in times of low seasons should always be your goal. And sometimes, I must say, debt accumulation is the result of operating under a closed heaven.

If you choose to live in disbelief and disobedience of God's divine principals for prosperity, you will never experience His best. If heaven is closed to you, then your life will have a yo-yo effect: up one day and down the next. And it can also be the result of robbing God in tithes and offerings. Living with accumulated debt is actually living in bondage to poverty. And poverty is a curse, but staying in it is a choice. Choose to honor God by *giving* your way out of poverty.

The Extract:

You have the power to break the curse of poverty in your life. Things will begin to turn around when you begin speaking to the mountains (obstacles of debt) and repent (change your mind) from mishandling money, especially the tithe, that really doesn't belong to you, but to God.

Sow your seed into good ground and expect a debt

cancellation harvest that also brings you increase. Start tithing faithfully on what you now have and earn. This will eventually result in a ground level of prosperity. You now have a chance to pay back what you owe, and you can rebuild your credit as you go. Rebuild your reputation with your creditors in order to do business with them and others in the future, and rebuild their trust in you as a person of integrity, one who fulfills obligations on or before the appointed due date. I mean, come on now, it's not only you and your reputation that's at stake here; it's about the survival of your family as well, if you have one.

Downsize in taste and leave the extravagant lifestyles for the rich and famous. Envision a life of freedom with your family. Recover quickly and leave a legacy for your children and your grandchildren and let this be your motivation to get completely out of debt, "owing no one anything but your love."

Joy Comes in the Morning

Just as financial ruin is not the end, neither is death the end. The pain of losing a loved one is indescribable at times; and it doesn't matter if it happened today, yesterday, or many years ago, you sometimes recall the last time you saw their face or heard their voice.

Grief tends to slip up on you sometimes catching you by surprise. And it resurfaces when your soul longs for sweet fellowship with the departed soul who's no longer held captive in their body. Even when reflecting on your fondest memories of them, the tears of sorrow will fill your eyes and stream down your cheeks. But this is not a bad thing. People we love become a part of us; however, when they depart this life, our hearts still feel them near. So our souls cry out for someone we emotionally feel yet cannot see or hear.

Be encouraged; it does get better after a while. The tears of grief will one day turn into gentle smiles, and then eventually become tears of joy and laughter as you reflect on their time spent here on earth. "Weeping may last through the night, but *joy comes with the morning"* (Psalm 30:5). Life says hello and it says goodbye, and it whispers goodbye to some people earlier than others. Celebrate the life they lived and use this as an antidote to sustain you during your unbearable time of grief.

The Loss of Loved Ones

The Loss of My Father

I will never forget my response when I got the news that my father had passed away. I became paralyzed with shock and ran into a nearby closet and wept profusely for a long period of time. To this day, I don't know why I chose a closet to find solace. Perhaps this happened because I wasn't very close to him and the reality of never seeing him again was overwhelming. There were things that I never got a chance to tell him due to hectic schedules and the distant miles between us. Plus too many years had gone by without me even reaching out to him with a simple phone call. Sadly enough, he died in the hospital without me being there for him.

On the day I arrived at his funeral, my heart was pounding like it was going to come out of my chest. I started shaking and weeping, and shifted completely out of control! That's when I realized that my heart was fractured into pieces because *my heart was filled with regret.* I regretted the fact that death took him before I got a chance to show him love—and not just say the words. It seemed as though no one was present in that little church but me, my father, and God. I was sick to my stomach and was an emotional wreck! And after all these years since his passing, I still can't fully describe how I felt inside on that day. "God blesses those who mourn, for they will be comforted" (Matthew 5:4).

Here's the life lesson that I learned: always make time for your family and the people you love! And try your best to verbalize your love and appreciation for them while they are alive! Once I returned home I was still emotionally discombobulated. But after a little while I was able to fully recover as my pleasant memories of him began to erase the pain of my loss. I saw him smiling and laughing with one tear rolling down his cheek, as always, and I even remembered the nick-name he gave me (don't ask, it's too funny, and it doesn't bear repeating now that I'm an adult), and then I thought of the genuine love that he had for all his children and how hard he worked in his business to provide for his children. This brought joy to my heart and a smile to my face. But the one thing that brought total healing to my heart was the fact that God used me to lead my own father in a prayer to receive salvation a few years before he passed away.

My loving father walked down the aisle to receive Christ's love and forgiveness in one of my meetings at the Marriott Hotel. I extracted the good out of my father's death by previously offering him the gift of eternal life — and he accepted! Out of all the times that I wasn't there for him, on that special occasion I didn't miss my divine appointment with him and his eternal destiny!

The Loss of My Mother, My Queen

My mother was an extraordinary woman. In my

opinion, my mother was an incredible humanitarian, who deeply loved God, her children, and *all* people. She received a healing miracle for Alzheimer's disease and lived to be eighty-seven years young.

As far back as I can remember, my mother was always very hospitable and had an abounding love for people outside of our family. She would give her last anything to meet the need of someone else. Her mentorship taught me much of what I know today. The day she died, I felt an *unusual void* in my life. And I mean a huge empty void. I remember thinking that I was alone in this world without her! I believe that the impact on my emotions was different with my mom's passing, because I was there at her bed-side two days before she was escorted into heaven. Her passing was more like *her long-awaited promotion* rather than a death. "The Lord cares deeply when His loved ones die" (Psalm 116:15).

Her home-going was more like a celebration than a grievous funeral. Not once did I weep or feel any of the emotions that I felt with my dad's passing. I believe it was because I always held her close to my heart, even with miles between us. She was my true role model and I loved and adored her. She was the sweetest person you ever wanted to meet. And she cherished her family. This lovely lady that I often called Queen gave birth to nine children—all by natural childbirth. To this day, I can't recall ever being left with a sitter as a child (or being left alone with anyone, for that matter), or going without two or three home cooked meals a day, etc. She aspired to become an author, but with nine children she never found the time to write. Taking care of us meant the world to her. And her entire adult life was spent building her world around us. Now, perhaps you understand why I didn't weep; there were too many pleasant memories of her for me to cry at that time.

At one point my heart was rejoicing for her as I unselfishly thought to myself, *After all she's done for her family and society, she deserves her eternal reward!* However, once I returned to my home, I found myself weeping like a little child. It dawned on me that I had lost the closest person to me in the world, the one person that I loved more than anyone else and the special gift from

God that could never be replaced. But once again, I was able to recall how God's grace and mercy was extended to my mother. I extracted the good out of my mother's death by previously leading her in a prayer for salvation many years before her passing, as well. Just as pressure is required to extract juice from fruits and vegetables, so must forced pressure (accepting the belief that loved ones are at rest in a better place) be used to extract the good from the passing away of loved ones.

New Life Beyond Abuse

Without question, God has a plan for your life that goes far beyond any abuse you may have suffered. The question is, do you believe that you were the cause of the abuse or that you deserved it for some strange reason? The last thing you want to do is blame yourself.

However, to get a much better understanding of the heart of an abuser and predator, let me illustrate: one early summer afternoon, the Anderson family was on their way to their favorite vacation resort, and while traveling, they had a car accident. Their dog was thrown from the car window and seriously injured. When the wife jumped out of the car to rescue him, the dog bit her. Now, after all those years of being their family pet, not once did he bite any member of their family, so why now?

You see, when you're hurting and in pain you lash out at anyone, whether you're a human or an animal. Hurt cries out for healing, but when it doesn't receive healing, it keeps on hurting and lashing out. Abusers and predators inflict pain because somewhere down the line, they too were abused. Nevertheless, it doesn't matter what a wounded person has gone through, no one deserves to be abused in any way.

Abuse is an atrocious violation against a person's body and soul. And like a violent storm, it sinks ships. You were supposed to have gone under in defeat. But let me enlighten you: the ultimate evil purpose for abuse is to break the spirit of a person in order to control and manipulate them. Abuse should be taken very seriously and dealt with. At the very first sign of it, help should be sought. Don't wait! You will never win the battle against any form of abuse without reporting it to your family, a trusted friend, or the authorities. To keep silent is to give power to the sadist and be marked and victimized for the rest of your life—even if that person is no longer in your life, and even if they are a total stranger.

Abuse comes in many forms: mental and emotional; verbal and physical; sexual; spiritual (often prevalent in some churches); and it even comes in the form of addictions and codependency. All forms of abuse are demonically imposed with the intent of destroying a person's true identity by turning a young girl or boy into a woman or man overnight, as well as influencing and altering their sexual preferences; by disfiguring the face of a beautiful woman to make her feel insecure and unattractive; by damaging the emotions of a person, making it hard for them to live and love again; and by using spiritual leadership to control and seduce wounded captives instead of helping them to recover. But look on the bright side: you are not the only one who's been abused.

I think at some point, everyone has experienced some form of abuse, anywhere from childhood to adulthood. So don't feel sorry for yourself, and don't be angry either. You were violated for a reason, and that reason may not have been revealed yet. In the meantime, allow your pain to become your pinnacle purpose and allow your pinnacle purpose to drive you forward, and while moving forward, help as many people as you can along the way.

Previously, you were a stagnant target, but right now you are becoming a moving force, and a moving force can't be hit very easily. Soon you will find the courage to confront the demons of your past and one day you will be given a voice to tell your story. "So the Levite took hold of his concubine and pushed her out the door. The men of the town abused her all night, taking turns raping her until morning. Finally, at dawn they let her go" (Judges 19:25).

To extract the good from abuse one must receive the new life that replaces the old, and you *must* forgive the violator, as well as yourself! This also includes learning to forget. Recognize that the forgiveness you need to extend and to receive is of a divine nature and cannot be achieved on this level without God's help. Every part of you will need to be healed and made new. "This means that anyone who belongs to Christ has become a new person. The old life is gone; a new life has begun" (II Corinthians 5:17)! And apart from this truth, I don't know of another road to freedom.

Running the Race Against Racism

Red, yellow, black, and white, I thought we all were precious in God's sight. Sadly, some of His creation doesn't always agree with this, and so our history of racism repeats itself. And although men died to bring freedom in times past, there's always a new generation that comes forth to keep racism alive.

Where did we get the notion that there are different races anyway? I beg to differ; there is only one race—the human race. Now, there are different dialects, skin pigments, and cultures in other continents, but still, we are the entire human race. "And *He has made from one blood every nation of men* to dwell on all the face of the earth, and has determined their pre-appointed times and the boundaries of their dwellings" (Acts 17:26).

When you begin *running the race against racism*, you will discover the true meaning of a disguised enemy called hatred. Racism is hatred. No person or group of another color is worthy enough to claim supremacy over another, at least not in God's eyes—and what His Word decrees is really all that matters.

Prejudice, on the other hand, is judgment in advance and is birthed out of a lack of understanding other cultures. This is what causes people to form unfavorable opinions beforehand of other people or unfair feelings of dislike for others simply because of the color of their skin (race), religion, sex, etc. Now, let's examine hatred and prejudice against *race and religion.*

Take the persecution of Christians and anti-Semitism for examples: During World War II, the Christians in Romania suffered under the Soviets and Nazis. Many Christians were severely beaten, imprisoned, massacred or forced into concentration camps with the Jews. Jewish people have been hated and tortured by their enemies, such as Hitler (the Nazis), as well as the modern day Hitlers, etc., and they have been emotionally bruised by "engrafted Gentiles" who believe in replacement theology, and who labeled them "Christ killers" out of ignorance. From ancient days to now, the mention or the sight of the cross is very painful for them. Instead of using the word *cross* they replace it with the word *tree.*

The Siege of Jerusalem took place in 1099, during the first Crusade. During this time, the Crusaders (bearing big *red crosses* on their armor and clothing) conquered the city from Egypt. The Siege is known for the horrific massacre that followed, during which time much of the population of Jerusalem was slaughtered—both Jew and Muslim—supposedly "in Christ's name." And albeit the cross is associated with Christ's atonement, to them, it's also associated with the brutal deaths of their people.

This damage can be turned around by offering them true repentance, love, and acceptance and an invitation to discover and accept their own Jewish Messiah. It has been said that the greatest form of anti-Semitism is withholding Christ from a Jew by refusing to share His love, forgiveness, and plan of salvation.

Christians have been persecuted for their beliefs as well. But Christians should be very cautious about judging and criticizing others, because I'm reminded that Sunday mornings (between 10:30am and 12:30pm) are the most segregated hours of the week. It appears that the United States has a church of every ethnicity: White, Black, Hispanic, Asian, etc., as well as a church of every denomination almost on every corner: Baptist, Methodist, Presbyterian, Catholic, Charismatic, Full Gospel, etc., and some are filled with people whose lives have never been changed and converted.

And don't forget what Muslims and Catholics have had to endure, such as all Muslims being stereotyped for the hate crimes of radical groups within their religion; and then of course, the Catholics have had to overcome the scandals and ridicule of all priest being stereotyped as child molesters due to the sins of other convicted priests, and the list goes on and on.

Additionally, let's examine the hatred and prejudice against the *sex of an individual.* In a man's world, you can easily find prejudice against women, both in corporate America and in the church. Women are not paid the same salaries as men in some professions, and they are often denied top level positions in the corporate world. Women are viewed as sex objects and are considered second-class citizens in many countries.

However, the one thing that's causing a stir, and is awakening the righteous indignation of so many today, is the prejudice against women in *Christendom* and in other religions. "For you are all children of God through faith in Christ Jesus. And all who have been united with Christ in baptism have put on Christ, like putting on new clothes. There is *no longer* Jew or Gentile, slave or free, *male and female.* For *you are all one* in Christ Jesus" (Galatians 3:26-28). Some religious leaders have embraced the fact that God chooses and uses whom He pleases. And now women are ordained as spiritual overseers.

Notwithstanding God's Holy Word, some religious

leaders still refuse to accept women in full leadership positions in the church. But ironically, the same women who are not allowed to speak or lead in Christendom and other religions are allowed and encouraged to *tithe their income* and become female *suicide bombers.*

And finally, there's the hatred against homosexuality and lesbianism. Now, because this is such a controversial subject, I approach it with sincere care and compassion. Young people who were secretively struggling with these issues have resorted to suicide because of the emotional pain of being hated and mistreated by others. This most certainly does break my heart! In fact, I am appalled when *anyone* is misused and/or abused in any form. Sometimes they are mocked and even physically attacked due to their lifestyles. *We shouldn't hate anyone for any reason.*

But what we should abhor is sin (all sin), as God does. These are precious individuals who believe that there was somewhat of a mix-up in their make-up (gender) while being conceived and manufactured. Others were sexually violated and now strongly believe that they have lost their identity. And then there are those who simply crave the affection of the same sex. I've talked to, and helped, many of them who felt trapped inside their bodies and wanted out. Instead of hate, you should offer them God's love and forgiveness. Listen to their story of what they may have experienced as a child, give them hope, and then tell them of God's *goodness!* "Or do you despise the riches of His goodness, forbearance, and longsuffering, not knowing that *the goodness of God leads you to repentance"* (Romans 2:4)?

Furthermore, racism is also the result of a child being fashioned to hate people who are different, and then becoming an adult who executes a plan to inflict the same racial sickness on others. I'm not quite sure if we'll ever see eye to eye on this issue, but I'm sure you will concur that we haven't totally arrived yet; however, we have indeed come a long way, at least in trying to coexist with one another.

An Asian man moved to the United States in hopes of fulfilling his dream of starting a business. He opened a Chinese restaurant and became very successful. One day before closing, he looked at that week's profits and said to his manager, "I don't like Blacks and I don't like Jews, but both Blacks and Jews sure like Chinese food!" I guess that means he's smiling all the way to the bank!

You see, everyone has a bit of "I don't like" in them, because we all are different. We must be patient with our progress against racism because our race is a marathon, not a sprint, and we are called by God to persevere. Not much time has passed, though, since the 18th, 19th, and early 20th centuries, when African Americans were lynched here in the United States, being strung up, shot, or both, and burned at the stake, maimed, dismembered, etc., without a trial for whatever they did or did not do, while the law did nothing.

Certainly, this was indeed an act of terror meant to dehumanize and terrorize all the African Americans and those who helped them, and to maintain control during the Jim Crow era. Gruesome photos of some of the victims were taken for distribution on postcards or in newspapers. Even the victim's body parts, including genitalia, were often distributed or put on public display.

History proves this era to be the Dark Ages for African Americans, both slaves and those who were considered "free", who survived such abysmal conditions.

We could ask God the pertinent question, why were extermination, sterilization, slavery and this brutality allowed? Even with His answer of truth, however, we still wouldn't fully comprehend the depths (the abyss) of racial hatred. But we must not ever forget the awesome power of God's infinite, redemptive love!

If God's redemptive love and *amazing grace* had the power to transform John Newton (a slave trader), surely He can continue to touch hearts today. However, the two most important things for us to remember are that *"love covers a multitude of sins"* (I Peter 4:8), and love conquers all! This is a new day, and it's time to move past the bitterness and pain of the past, if you haven't already. There are so many wonderful people in this world who are not guilty of the sins of their ancestors, and therefore they should not be blamed and charged for them.

There is positively no other way to extricate good from prejudice and racial hatred, except by offering in exchange *divine forgiveness and unrestricted love without retaliation!* This is true because there's no greater force than forgiveness; and there's no greater power than love!

Chapter 7

LIVING THE GOOD LIFE

Misery is a mental state of suffering caused by hardship, affliction, calamity, privation, curses, catastrophe, poverty, and all forms of abuse. This state of mind has the power to invite even more trouble than what's mentioned here. Being locked into this mental state will take away your desire to fight and to win in life. Therefore rising above adverse circumstances to enjoy a life offering exceptionally good things will require your permission.

You must desire to be free from misery before you can ever experience freedom. The good that can be extracted out of life is there waiting for you to obtain it. When you want freedom badly enough, simply grant yourself the permission and your entire miserable environment will change. Then you will discover the *peace of mind* that finally comes when you're able to pay your bills on or before the due date; walk in divine health; have a fulfilling, long-lasting marriage; raise God-fearing children; own a successful business; and live debt-free, to name a few.

Believe it or not, there are some people who actually live this way, and you should be one of them! But this will only happen if you agree to this kind of lifestyle as the will of God for your life. This transformation is predicated on one thing: your decision. Change your old mind-set from feeling unworthy or perhaps guilty for your promotion, to a mind-set of agreement and acceptance of it. But remember, changing your mind-set requires the total rejection of what other people think, say, and do, especially if their previous input influenced the wrong choices you made, and if their current input contradicts your new change.

When I think of the word good, I think of what's beneficial and morally right. Everything in life that's defined as good is not always morally right. Infidelity may feel good to some people and provide for them a temporary means of escape, but it's not morally right. There are many other people who choose to have sexual intimacy with partners while living together to prevent marrying the wrong person—this, too, is not morally right. And everything you deem to be good is not always beneficial for you.

So instead of just receiving the "good" out of life, be sure to receive only what's beneficial and morally right. Of course, eating the right food is good for your health, but overeating is not beneficial. In fact, it can lead to obesity, certain diseases, and even death. And last, but certainly not least, fasting is good for the soul, but going too long without nutrients is not beneficial for your body. Maintaining a balance in life is a key to experiencing longevity.

Before I make any decisions, or receive anything or anyone into my life, I try to remember to ask myself the question, "Will I, along with others, benefit from this?" Because if not, then I'm wasting my time with it, and time is the one thing that's nonredeemable. I also try to use caution when accepting all the overwhelming good in order to prevent greed. Sometimes I even reflect on my humble beginnings to keep me content and appreciative of what I already have.

James grew up in poverty and developed a poverty mentality that hindered everything he set out to do. He was abandoned by his father and became very bitter toward the world. He had a speech impediment and could barely read and write. After years of struggling through grade school, which he hated, he managed to enter high school with a low GPA.

However, James was indeed a "born athlete", as many would say. So while in high school, he received a scholarship to play basketball at a well-known college out of state. But something changed about James before he graduated and entered college—he no longer had a speech impediment. And it was later revealed, the low GPA was the result of him not caring about anything or anyone, including himself. To him, life had no meaning.

Surprisingly, James wasn't ignorant at all. He was actually quite intelligent. And this was something that his own mother didn't know about him. He simply didn't like going to school and the hand that life had dealt him. And apparently, what he wanted and needed the most was love and affirmation from his father. His instructors would look down and shake their heads after confronting him regarding his low grades. But nothing they said moved him, because he had no will to fight— or to succeed, for that matter.

Eventually, he began to pour himself into his studies and graduated with a 3.90 GPA. Then he went off to college. But instead of being manipulatively passed on through college, he graduated with high honors. And to the surprise of so many who knew him, his degree was in the field of medicine. This baffled even more people who thought he would become a "professional ball player."

James beat all the odds and chose to get all the good out of a bad situation. He changed his mind-set in order to succeed but always remembered his humble beginnings. He overcame his hardships and built strong character from swimming against the current. Then he used education as a key to unlock possibilities. Finally, as a medical doctor, he's now enjoying the good life.

Change for the good sends many people straight to the top, because the bottom level of poverty is massively over-crowded. The ability to *rise above it all* is already within you, as it was with James. You are who you are becoming. And one day I hope you will discover that it's more important to become someone than it is to strive to become something.

A More Powerful Witness

In this society we live in, you will become a more powerful witness when you can actually display God's acts of kindness and what His prosperity looks like. And with an economy that's taken a downturn—a financial collapse, if you will—His provision for you will serve as a beacon to many who have lost their way. It will also provoke some people to godly jealousy, while provoking others to envy and hatred. But know this: having good things in life is not the same as enjoying the good life.

Some of my acquaintances often express to me their misery and how they wish they'd never inherited their wealth, or obtained it by greed or hard labor. They resent the fact that what they have cannot buy them health and happiness. And after a while, some regret having the awesome responsibility of managing it. Trust me, it can be a major headache at times.

Nevertheless, we need money to live here on earth, so we make do. However, money can never fill the void of a lust for people, power, and things in you—only God can do that. The void is what He created for Himself in the first place. Furthermore, we also live in a society where poor people are not acknowledged or accepted. This reminds me of Solomon's words of wisdom: "Here is another bit of wisdom that has impressed me as I have watched the way our world works.

There was a small town with only a few people, and a great king came with his army and besieged it. A *poor, wise man* knew how to save the town, and so it was rescued. But afterward no one thought to thank him. So even though wisdom is better than strength, those who are wise will be *despised if they are poor.* What they say will not be appreciated for long" (Ecclesiastes 9:13-16).

In other words, you may be as wise as Solomon, but if you live in poverty, people will glean from your wisdom and despise you at the same time. If this is the case with you, then stop for a moment and count your "friends" who listen to what your life *now* speaks. Come on, let's be truthful. They are not listening to you. And this is because poverty is not a good witness, therefore it has no voice. If you've experienced major setbacks and you no longer have the wealth, most of them may have already left you.

On the other hand, having wealth, be it new money or old, is all that's required for your voice to be heard in some circles. If you possess this power of having money, then use it to your advantage and for God's glory. But whatever you do, don't forget to honor God with all of your success, and when you need help in times of trouble, He will be there for you and He'll increase you even more. "Honor the Lord with your wealth and with the best part of everything you produce. Then he will fill your barns with grain, and your vats will overflow with good wine" (Proverbs 3:9, 10).

Long gone are the days of fictitious humility and being poverty stricken, and long gone should be the days for bringing ridicule upon your household with accumulated bad debt. Whoever said that living in poverty honors the Creator of heaven and earth, who owns it all and created it all for His good pleasure and for us to enjoy. Surely they didn't read this in His Word. No one wants to serve someone—and that includes the Creator—who can't provide for them. So to prevent the world from viewing Him this way, He wants to lavishly provide for you. But to fully comprehend and receive God's provision, you'll have to renounce the false doctrine that's associated with prosperity. It's the doctrine that hoards without truly propagating His message. Accepting the truth regarding this subject will free you to serve God and not "mammon" and will make you a trustworthy steward and witness for Him. This is His optimal and ultimate plan.

Mike and Kathy met and married at the young ages of nineteen and twenty-one. They both were in college at the time and decided to complete their education—and so they did. Once they graduated, they found good-paying jobs and started their lives together. Mike was a hard-working man who made good money but was very capricious with it. Throughout their marriage, Kathy was used to hearing him say, "You'll have to take care of this; I don't have any money left over." Kathy, however, was frugal with her spending and managed money very well. She paid half the bills and always paid them on time. She made sure they tithed ten percent of their income to their local church and faithfully gave special love offerings to help feed the poor. She dressed modestly and was happy in her own skin. In other words, Kathy refused to make a big fuss over her outward appearance or competing with others to impress with material things. She was content with her life.

But twenty years later, life took an unexpected turn.

Mike had a severe heart attack that almost took his life. After he recovered a bit and made plans to return to his work, he suffered a mild stroke and experienced partial paralysis on the left side of his body. At forty-one years young, Mike was unable to work and care for himself. And because he spent money as fast as he could make it, he had no money saved. But Mike and everyone else were clueless regarding Kathy's excellent stewardship. Due to the magnitude of Mike's illnesses, they went years without Mike's salary to help sustain them, but for some strange reason, Mike never heard Kathy complain about the bills piling up.

Kathy had saved and invested most of her money very wisely for twenty years. She also had received an inheritance, which was a substantial amount of money, after her father's death. I believe they call this "she money!" This put Kathy in a different position: before, she went without the "pleasures" of life, and now she could pay cash for anything she desired. But most importantly, during their time of crisis, Kathy had secretly acquired enough money for both of them to retire at early ages.

Mike finally recovered after much therapy, and after changing his eating habits. Subsequently, Mike learned a lot about life from his near-death experience because it changed him in a universal way.

In the end, Mike and Kathy became *a more powerful witness* to everyone they knew and met. And Kathy, due to her selfless lifestyle, her loyalty to tithing and sowing, and her sincere love for her husband, was able to purchase a new beach-front vacation home in Hawaii, where they spent most of their time together—*living the good life.*

CHAPTER 8

EXPERIENCING THE
ABUNDANT LIFE

Would you agree that experiencing and living the abundant life has been *overrated?* Perhaps the misconceived ideas regarding this subject are the reason. It appears that these ideas were propagated and only those who taught it benefited from it, and not you. So let me approach abundant living from a different angle that will include you.

The lifestyles of royal families in a monarchy, or the rich and famous will always exhibit extravagant wealth.

And whether people approve of it or not, wealth and prominence go with the territory. However, not everyone is born into the families of the rich and famous, or into a royal family under a monarchial government. Some people are born into poverty. But it doesn't matter which category you fall under, whether rich or poor, it has no influential effect on your destiny. Why? It's simple. The destination plans of both categories can change in an instant.

A person born into wealth can mismanage money, die prematurely without a successor, be found guilty in a scandal, etc., and thereby bring down an empire and lose everything. In contrast, the person born into poverty can use being poverty-stricken as a force to drive them to succeed. And albeit the journey to becoming wealthy may be long and hard, the driving force of lack makes it possible to attain. In the end we search for both characters and find one who succeeded and the other who failed. One relied on the sufficiency of what was already established and the other relied on the *hope* of one day having.

An investment banker had two sons that worked closely with him in his firm. Out of the two sons, the eldest, nonchalantly held his position with the company, and it was rumored that he often spoke against it. When the time arrived for bonuses to be distributed, the eldest son asked for and received, in advance, his bonus of a large amount. He took time off to enjoy traveling, etc. But after lavishly spending, partying, and living it up, he became very ill and had to return home early.

Once he fully recovered, he returned to work and sarcastically asked his father, "Why didn't you come to greet me with a welcome back celebration, kill the fatted calf, put a ring on my finger, and place a robe on my shoulders?" His father replied, "Number one, you are not the prodigal; number two, you were not lost and therefore you have not been found; number three, you spent your bonus, but I'm sure—due to your conniving—you have money in reserve; number four, I hope your future has a better forecast, because you are no longer employed at this firm."

Some people are masters at squandering the wealth of

others. However, experiencing and living the abundant life begins with your outlook on life and how you value it. Your *need* should press you forward with a purpose to achieve either sufficient or abundant living. But guard against self-sufficiency because it breeds conceit and complacency and causes you to waste time and money, simply because you can. It also causes you to stop the production of your success by stopping to smell the roses one time too many. And while you have your life on pause, your impoverished opponent becomes your counterpart who gains momentum, surpasses you, and finishes the race.

Perhaps now you understand why your beginning doesn't always predict your final outcome. It's always best to remain humble, no matter your status in life. "If you think you are standing strong, be careful not to fall" (I Corinthians 10:12). This means don't flaunt or boast about what you possess or what you've become, and most importantly, don't allow flattery to inflate your ego, because while doing so, you could experience a humiliating fall.

My understanding of true abundance helps me to envision having the excess that not only supplies my needs and wants, but also overflows to the needs of others. So in essence, when I think of abundant living, I think of *charitable giving!* People who live in abundance generally have very generous hearts. "I have come that they may have life, and that they might have it more abundantly" (John 10:10). In Greek[1] the word *abundantly* is "perissos", which means superabundant (in quantity) or superior (in quality); by implication excessive; over and above, more than enough; overflow.

It's very apparent to me that the original plan was for us to live a *superior life* in *superabundance.* Superior is not just a high standard of living, it's the pinnacle, and superabundance is not just having enough, it's having an amount that can't be measured. So instead of operating in the red, you stay in the black; instead of being in debt, you sometimes pay in full; and instead of running out, you always have a supply! You will no longer live in distress when you live in the overflow blessing, and when your life is excessively enriched, people will desire to know your success story. (You will exemplify what it means to experience God's abundance.)

The abundant lifestyle will most definitely speak without you saying a word. This lifestyle was provided for all, but not all are knowledgeable of it or willing to receive it. These are two of the main reasons many don't possess it. So from this moment on, you must make the decision to accept what was provided for you. God is not going to bankrupt heaven by pouring out His abundance on you. It's His will to prosper you in every aspect of your life. When your needs are met—because you have more than enough—you will have peace.

However, the Scripture places emphasis on having *life in abundance,* and not just on possessing things. The Greek[2] word for *life* is "zoe", which means in the sense of existence, life, in an absolute sense and without end. And life, i.e., blessed life, life that satisfies. This is the true meaning of *experiencing the abundant life*—having a peaceful life that satisfies here on earth, and having eternal life at the end of this life. Having material abundance is not everything, but having eternal security is.

Soul Prosperity

According to some of the doctrines that are taught, prosperity is something that you say, and call forth, all at the same time. But let's not confuse the power of our confession with the magical Law of Attraction. You will attract what you say, and there's no doubt about that, but attracting wealth without soul prosperity to manage it wisely, and properly disperse it, is like putting money in pockets with holes in them. What a person attracts, they'll not always keep. "I pray that you may prosper in all things and be in health, just as your *soul prospers*" (III John 2). This is the perfect balance.

The soul is the seat of the senses, passions, affections, appetites, and desires, and is considered to be the lower aspect of a person's nature. This is what governs your actions. So quite clearly, this part of you should prosper and be disciplined as you excel.

If you were to receive a million dollars right now and your mind had not been reconditioned to think and operate like a millionaire, what would you do with it? If you received it and your *will* was set on just your good pleasure—and not God's, what would you do with it? And if you received it and your *emotions* were completely out of balance (spontaneous, emotional spender), what would you do with it?

My point is this, riches can flee the same way they arrive sometimes, and many people become worse off than before due to the mismanagement of money and the insurmountable accumulation of debt. When an emotional, spontaneous spender receives increase, their first desire is to impress others with it—without being conscious of it. There's just something about going without for so long that makes you want to have it all when given the chance.

All too often emotional spenders spend money on themselves without thinking and without even counting the cost. Other times they splurge on others to win admiration and acceptance. However, if you go back to their childhood, the character they now exhibit is the character (appetites, dreams, and fantasies) they had as a child. Whoever you are in character and whatever you are driven to do before you receive abundance will only be magnified afterward.

It's similar to a man who's struggling with lust. When he finds himself in a pool of temptation, surrounded by beautiful women, his true character will manifest. And instead of remembering that he already has a beautiful wife at home, he indulges and then puts his mistress up in a penthouse apartment. Surely you're not alarmed by this, because it happens wherever there's greed and a lust for power, etc. Indulging was in his character to begin with. Possessing wealth while being bound by lust simply made it easier for him to act out his fantasies without having to count the cost.

The abundant life should coincide with a person's *soul* being in subjection to God's will being carried out— and not the lust of the flesh being fulfilled. However, receiving and living in abundance on any level will not happen, if your soul has not progressed and aligned itself with His purpose for the use of money.

Allowing Hate to Motivate and Elevate

I'm sure you are quite aware that opposition and even jealous hatred is associated with living the abundant life. And if you seek to please people, then the abundant life is not for you. Some people will envy and always have an opinion of what's best for your life, because they believe they know more about you than you do. There are even times when your abundant blessings will cause people who knew you "when" to break communications with you, especially those who shared in your small amount of success in the beginning. And when you rose to the top and out-grew them and your little comfort zone, they began to hate. But hate should not be underestimated.

You can achieve more success and go even higher by *allowing hate to motivate and elevate.* People are so amusing when they are deceived by jealous hatred. (This is very humorous to me!) Haters harm only themselves. The damage to them is similar to a person taking a dose (45 mg) of strychnine poison and hoping the person they hate dies. The good that can be extracted out of jealous hatred is the power that motivates and elevates you. This should be used to make you an even greater witness.

Another positive thing we all should remember is that your *haters* also serve as your *elevators,* who bring just enough free publicity to send you straight to the *penthouse.* Thank you so much for my promotion! You see, motivation is one thing and elevation is another. You need more than just motivation to get somewhere—you need help getting there. And elevation does just that. Oh my goodness, the power of elevation launches!

Possessing this type of mind-set will encourage your heart when the negativity is a bit too much. And it will also help you to overlook the ignorance of others who foolishly say and do things that could potentially hurt you and your reputation. (But sometimes people are under the influence of evil, and they know exactly why they are conspiring against you.)

Billy Graham was scheduled to share a message with the world on November 7, 2013. This day of releasing his "last message" was also the day of his 95th birthday. But news had spread earlier that week that Billy Graham had passed away. However, it was confirmed that this was a complete death hoax, and one of many that are related to celebrities. The rumors spread the day before his big event, and a *'R.I.P. Billy Graham'* Facebook page attracted close to one million 'likes,' along with their condolences. More than likely, this may have brought even more publicity leading up to his event. But lessons were learned as people began to realize that news of his death had not been broadcast on major networks in America, which was a red light indicator that this rumor must have been fictitious.

Clearly the death of a person of this stature would be breaking news across networks in America as well as worldwide. On November 7, 2013, via the medium of television, Billy Graham celebrated his birthday in North Carolina with his family and friends from around the world. This goes to show that you can't always believe what you read and hear in the media and on Facebook pages—and this includes all forms of *gossip!*

Extravagant Living

Perhaps we should pause and define extravagance and then compare it to abundance. Extravagant living is a lifestyle of excessive squandering and exorbitant spending. Abundance, however, is having more than enough of whatever you need and desire. Try not to confuse the two when desiring to live a much better life. Extravagant living can also be associated with greed, insecurity, and emotional pain.

When you've been deeply wounded or traumatized and then you're removed from that environment, you sometimes develop a syndrome, and you realize that somewhere along the line you lost your identity. God created us to be loved and accepted by one another, and when these two attributes are absent in relationships, we feel demoralized, and then we seek after human creature comforts.

Perhaps you've been there or know of someone who's there now: living extravagantly, yet they're hurting so very deeply inside. Bad relationships leave people so devastated at times. Whichever the case, this is not the time to dissociate yourself from them. In this kind of crisis, you'll either need them or be needed—now more than ever. Be very cautious not to allow their wealth and their outward family success stories to intimidate you— if your lifestyle doesn't reflect the same.

Remember, in some cases, it's a united front that's established to impress. Too often, it's also a cover-up for worry, anxiety, and fear associated with infidelity in a marriage. Now, am I implying that you shouldn't have a lot of money and material possessions, or desire to have them? Of course not! I am acquainted with many prominent, wealthy people, who are some of the most reserved and down-to-earth people you could meet. Some of them are philanthropists, who invest money to help the poor and needy of society. However, what I am saying is that having wealth doesn't define you as a person, and it definitely doesn't fill the human void; but it certainly does make it easier for you to hoard things and hide personal pain.

Yolanda was an assertive, successful business-woman

who was married to a highly educated and intelligent man named Stan. He too was successful in business and was well-known in their community. Stan loved his wife dearly and always expressed it through gift giving. Stan and Yolanda had two children and lived in one of the largest estates in their community. Due to their level of success, they were envied by so many people who pretended to be their friends. "The poor is hated even of his own neighbor: but the rich hath many friends" (Proverbs 14:20).

However, having money will attract all kinds of people. Their curious and watchful neighbors were not surprised to see Yolanda in an exotic new car that Stan bought her practically every two years. He insisted on buying her the most extravagant jewelry for every gala event they attended. They were always gone on vacation to some exotic place, and when seen in public they looked happily married and in love with each other, and even their children appeared to be happy. Without a doubt, this was the ideal couple and family most women only dream of.

One day Stan's expression of love arrived at their home in the form of beautiful red roses — 120, to be exact. "Stan, the roses are beautiful, but why did you buy so many?" Yolanda asked with excitement.

"Well, it's because you deserve them and more!" Stan replied. As always, another amazing gift of love was received and greatly appreciated.

The next day, Yolanda received a call on their house phone. She answered it, "Hello, this is Yolanda," but the caller remained silent on the line. Yolanda held the receiver away from her ear, bit her bottom lip, and once again said, "Hello!"

And then there was a response: "This is not someone you know, obviously, but I'm calling for Stan."

"May I ask who's calling?" Yolanda asked.

The caller said, "It really doesn't matter anymore, because the four-month affair that I had with Stan is over, but I still feel connected to him! I'm very depressed right now. So, that's why I'm calling. Is he there?"

"Excuse me!!! This is his wife that you're talking to!" Yolanda said.

"Stan never told me he was married! He told me that if I ever needed to call him, I could, and he said if a woman ever picked up, that would be his maid."

Heartbroken and extremely infuriated, Yolanda was able to put the scattered pieces of the puzzle together: the 120 beautiful red roses were her husband's guilt compensation for the four-month (120 day) affair that he was having with the scorned, indiscreet woman. After many long nights of weeping on her pillow, suffering from depression, and displaying outbursts of anger, Yolanda decided to take the *united front* way out of this painful situation. This was her choice because she loved him, and because too much had been invested in her twenty-five year marriage: all the money, the kids, etc.

However, Stan carried on with his business as usual because Yolanda refused to hold him accountable, to give him an ultimatum, and to seek counseling. He refused to repent of his conduct and continued in his lifestyle of infidelity with other women. And there you have it: not everything that shines brightly is gold, and not everything that sparkles is a genuine diamond or

crystal—and so it is with the false pretense of successful
extravagant living!

Chapter 9

THE AUTHENTIC GOOD

An atheist named Tom was a bestselling author, and a man who lived his entire life in spiritual disbelief. One day he became deathly ill and was hospitalized. The pain caused by his disease was excruciating, and night after night the surrounding patients in the hospital heard him yelling and swearing, repeatedly. One night the pain was so intense that he forgot his disbelief in God and began to curse God. After hearing this, those patients who were acquainted with him began to question why an atheist, who doesn't believe that God exists, would acknowledge Him with cursing. Many believed that God must have revealed Himself to him and presented an invitation for him to ask for and receive the forgiveness of his sins.

Shortly after all the swearing finally subsided, the atheist shouted, *"It's too late, it's too late, it's too late! I cannot change the way I was raised to believe!"* But he wasn't talking to his family who were present there in the room. Then he released a blood-curdling, unusually high-pitched scream that was heard throughout the entire floor of that hospital. Tom died having rejected God on his death bed. No one slips into eternity without experiencing God, at least once.

The Authentic Good came down to save and receive the atheist, but the atheist was locked into a mind-set that totally rejected God in this life and the life that was to come. Those who were gathered at his bedside said that before he took his last breath, he acknowledged seeing *pitched-black darkness* and burning *flames of fire.* This was believed to be the reason why he began screaming before he died. "Finally, the poor man died and was carried by the angels to be with Abraham. The rich man also died and was buried, and his soul went to the place of the dead. There, in torment, he saw Abraham in the far distance with Lazarus at his side. The rich man shouted, Father Abraham, have some pity! Send Lazarus over here to dip the tip of his finger in water and cool my tongue. I am in anguish in these *flames*" (Luke 16:22-24).

You can believe and live your life as you choose, but one day, in the end, you will indeed meet your Maker! Let now be the time for you to place value on your life, by making the Authentic Good the head of your life. All the finer things in life can't compare to what will happen the day you make this choice. The atheist took none of his wealth with him, only his lost soul. The wealth was left for others to disperse among themselves. And the legacy of doubt and unbelief continued in his family.

Your mind-set is one of the strongest powers of persuasion you possess. And this substantiates the fact that not even God Himself can change your mind for you, even at the point of death. You are a free moral agent with the power to accept or reject Him and the eternal life that He gives. Decide now, because tomorrow always seems to be too late. The only good that could possibly come out of this heart-wrenching life lesson is the fact that this doesn't have to be you. We learn from other people's mistakes. But we should spend a lifetime learning from what life has taught us, is teaching us, and shall continue to teach us, of its complex meaning.

The Authentic Good gives everyone a chance to begin and end life correctly. I'm sure this is sobering enough for you to appreciate how blessed you are to be alive and reading this about someone else. The counterfeit, the camouflage, and everything that disguises is what most of us have experienced in our lives—and then there's the authentic.

Only that which comes from above can be classified as authentic good and everlasting. Everything else in life can only provide a temporary thrill. "Whatever is good and perfect comes down to us from God our Father, who created all the lights in the heavens. He never changes or casts a shifting shadow" (James 1:17).

I want you to take note of the words *"good and perfect," "comes down to us,"* and *"Father."* Quite clearly, we see that God the Father is The Authentic Good, who operates in and through our lives here on earth. In fact, He's the reason for our total existence. Experiencing a life of abundance without God at its center is worthless and void of the true meaning of the abundant life. There is no life apart from Him. And absolutely nothing good ever comes out of life unless it is given to us by Him.

Think of the air you breathe, the rain that falls, the sun that warms, and the water you drink—all provided by God the Father. Yet day after day, some people refuse to acknowledge His existence, and they fail to appreciate His plentiful blessings.

The Purpose of Pain and Suffering

Is the universal language of pain a *friend* or a *foe?* Pain is actually an indication that something is wrong in the physical body, and without this indicator many people would die from a silent killer. Likewise, personal pain reveals what's prevalent or deficient in our character. The character unveils the disposition of a person when faced with tragedy, trials, temptation, etc. It is also the make-up of a person that determines whether or not they will survive an ordeal or fall apart. I believe that the personal pain of *all* life's challenges is allowed for the main purpose of revealing our mandate in life and our destiny.

No one reaches their destiny without first traveling a predestined pathway, and often this pathway includes pain and suffering. Life would be trite and there would be no forward movement without difficulties. When we are faced with a trial, it somewhat stagnates us when we spend too much time searching for answers and remedies. This method of dealing with problems causes you to magnify the problem rather than the deliverance. My point is this: once you experience pain, *the proper way to process it* is to discover its purpose.

Release the pain therapeutically, allow the process of healing to begin and then keep moving onward. Don't allow it to isolate you and hold you captive. Life is a tour and it is similar to going on a tour with a tour guide. We visit places in life, but we don't remain there. Sometimes it's needful and very important for us to explore our past, our present, and our future, but we should avoid encamping around an experience, especially if it was painful. You build on a platform if it is conducive, but not around it. This applicable truth will alter the outcome of all your experiences and will paradigm shift or quantum leap you to another phase, level, or dimension in life.

When a pregnant woman is in labor, the pain can be absolutely unbearable, but as soon as her child is born she forgets what the pain felt like because she experiences astonishing joy. Remember, *pain doesn't last forever; it comes and it goes, and it always precedes giving birth.* "A woman, when she is in labor, has sorrow because her hour has come; but as soon as she has given birth to the child, she no longer remembers the anguish, for joy that a human being has been born into the world" (John 16:21). Change your outlook on life and view what you're going through as a catalyst for giving birth to something life-changing and new. Try not to waste precious time questioning God about why He allowed your pain and suffering. Focus on the *promotion* associated with enduring until the end and on coming out of your adverse circumstances.

Shelby was a strong-willed fifteen-year-old who got pregnant by a man in his thirties. This wasn't considered a rape case because it happened with her consent. Shelby was physically and sexually abused by her father at the age of eight and became sexually active and matured very quickly for her age. As soon as she discovered that she was pregnant, she became paralyzed with fear and went to an abortion clinic to do what the child molester said to do: "Take care of this…I'll pay for it!"

Shelby nervously arrived at the clinic, confused and with two main questions in her mind: *God, you saw what my father did to me as a little girl: why do you allow so many fathers to get away with physically and sexually abusing their children? And why do people accept what they've done and act like it never happened?* While she was waiting, feeling alone and hopeless, she began to cry as she recalled the trauma of her abuse. Suddenly, she ran out of the clinic and went home and told her mother everything that had happened to her, including the physical and sexual abuse by her father. Together they wept uncontrollably in each other's arms and released countless years of personal pain. Then Shelby fell on the floor into a fetal position and screamed as if being beaten.

Later that evening, her mother was able to convince her to not have the abortion, but to give the child up for adoption to a couple that couldn't have children. She verbally agreed, but nothing was concrete. Eight months later she gave birth to a little girl. Now, the policy was to remove the child immediately after birth, without the mother seeing the child, to prevent bonding. As they took the child away, Shelby yelled, "Wait! I want to see my child!" She looked into the eyes of that precious little one and began to weep, and she refused to let her go. She held on to her very tightly, stroked her face and hair, and kissed her repeatedly. And then, across the face of an abused and broken young girl came this "you light up my life" smile.

Just as the Authentic Good is present at death (the close of life), so is He present at birth (the beginning of new life). It was God's presence that filled the room that day and gave her a change of heart, because *He is the giver of life!* "The Lord gave me this message: '"I knew you before I formed you in your mother's womb. Before you were born I set you apart and appointed you…"'" (Jeremiah 1:4, 5). Shelby and her mother raised this little girl, who became an intelligent, vivacious young woman who later graduated from an Ivy League school.

When you contemplate having an *abortion,* always remember, *there is an alternative.* Another embryo could have been destroyed, but due to a wise choice, another innocent life was spared that time. Shelby and her mother's pain and suffering revealed the love in their hearts to unselfishly give life and not take it away. They both chose to forgive and to demonstrate love in return for the abuse. These were tough life lessons to learn, but Shelby, with the help of her mom, conquered defeat.

All of the personal pain that we experience in life falls under the category of *purpose opportunities.* Once these challenges make known the reason for your pain, they then present to you the opportunity to change your circumstances and to make a positive impact on the lives of others. This leads me to believe that *pain, both physical and personal (but exclusive of all abuse), comes to us as a friend* and brings with it warning signs for the help that we need. This is *the purpose for pain and suffering.*

Renée was a single parent and a loving mother to her son Christopher. She was told by physicians that she would never bear another child due to a disease she had contracted. As her son approached his 14th birthday, she discovered that her son was ill but managed to hide it because he loved to stay in his room, eat junk food, and play video games. He was a very isolated child and didn't talk much. Whenever Renée would ask him how he was doing, his response would be, "I'm good, Mom." And that's it.

One morning Christopher woke up screaming at the top of his lungs. Renée rushed into his room and found him dead by the side of his bed. To her dismay, she was told that Christopher died instantly of an aneurysm that occurs in preteens and adolescents. Renée became suicidal when the reality of her greatest loss—her only child and the inability to have another one set in. Many people believe that no parent should have to bury a child, because children should bury their parents. And some say, "There's no pain like the loss of a child!"

After going out one evening, she started drinking alcohol and began to display uncouth behavior. When it was time to leave, she refused to be driven home by her friend, so she left the restaurant alone and headed home. Minutes later, Renée had a car accident: she ran into the back of an SUV at a stop light. The man in the vehicle wasn't hurt, and neither was she. He got out of his truck and quickly approached her car. Renée had sobered up a bit and was afraid that the man might do her bodily harm. When he reached her car, he looked at her and began to laugh, and then he said to her, "Are you okay?"

"Yes I am, and you?" she replied.

"I'm fine, thank you!" he said. Then, while exchanging information and waiting for the police to arrive, the man told her why he was laughing. He began to share with her how his wife had died two years previously without giving him children. He said he told God, during his time of grief, "I will never look for love again, and the only way I would even consider dating again would be if the right person *ran into me*" (a metaphor meaning "… *approached me*")! Then he said, "This was the first thing that came to mind when you hit me; and of course when I saw you, I couldn't help but laugh!"

At that very moment, Renée was thinking, *If he only knew…!* Shortly afterward the police arrived, and John, and Renée were both laughing and enjoying each other's company. As it turned out, John was a humble Doctor of Psychology, who didn't wear his Ph.D. badge on his chest all the time, but was well equipped to help Renée with all of her past traumatic experiences.

One year later they were married and made plans for adopting children. Eight months later, Renée became pregnant with their first child — so they thought. But they later discovered that she was carrying twins (something that ran in his family). "With men this is impossible, but with God all things are possible" (Matthew 19:26). Both John and Renée experienced the death of a loved one and were without children until Renée gave birth to strong and healthy twins: a handsome baby boy and a beautiful baby girl. When the twins were born, John wept and couldn't seem to stop weeping. Once they arrived home with their newborns, John took Renée in his arms and kissed her very passionately. He then served her day and night until she fully recovered. Renée's physicians said no to the possibility of a second childbirth; but *The Authentic Good*, who always has the final word, said yes!

THE FINAL WORD

What Do You Want Out of Life?

It is quite refreshing to complete a good book, and I hope you enjoyed this one and found yourself engaged in it to the end. Perhaps by now I have your full attention after taking a closer look at the lives of many different people from many different angles. I believe that you're ready now to make the right decisions regarding your life, your future. But to do this, you must first decide what you really want out of life.

And I can't think of a better time to do this than now. The good success of tomorrow hinges on what you plan and prepare for today. Without a doubt, my message is speaking to you right now and has shed light on the many dimensions of your life that may have remained *hidden* and *unaddressed*.

In our pursuit to live a better life we caught a glimpse of the state and condition of our minds in *The Mind Trap;* we discovered our need for a transformation in *Embracing Change;* we conquered the fear of the unknown in *Enjoying The Journey of Life;* we took a closer look at the importance of putting first things first in *Prioritizing Life;* we witnessed the power of bringing order back into our lives in *Order Out of Chaos;* we learned the purpose for pressure in *Extracting The Good;* we accepted the right to guiltlessly enjoy life in *Living The Good Life;* we now understand the dire need for developing good character in *Experiencing The Abundant Life;* and we saw The Source of life in *The Authentic Good*. We are given the knowledge of the truth to equip us to do something about what's out of balance or out of control in our lives.

However, when you receive the truth, you become accountable for what you now know. And when truth is not put into practice, it becomes dormant and good for nothing—and no part of your life will change. Perhaps you couldn't imagine how extricating *good* from pain and affliction, betrayal, infidelity, opposition, persecution, and trauma could be possible—or how others could triumph over these obstacles.

So the question you must ask yourself is this: *"What should I do with the multiplicity of choices that are presented to me (the many ways of seeing and accepting the good part of life that's outweighed and hidden by all the bad)?"* Then you must answer it for yourself, realizing that deep down inside, you already know the answer. Your answer is there, because your daily frustrations and occasional comments about *"being tired of the way things are"* give it away. They also reveal the fact that, if you could, you most certainly would change things. Now, with help from this book, you will continue to be inspired, coached, and empowered to start turning things around to *get the good out of life,* for once in your life!

APPRECIATION

These are the last important words that I typed upon completion of this book, because I couldn't find words more powerful than *thank you* to express my gratitude to all the wonderful people who helped make this book possible. From my family, staff, editors, graphic designer, and every other contributor to every single blog reader, who faithfully read, offer your encouragement, share a post with a friend, and invite others to join us at www.getthegoodoutoflife.com, to the Authentic Good, who makes all things possible—my thanks! From the heart I thank, and deeply love, each of you!

Notes

Chapter 1: The Mind Trap

1. Jerome Carson and Elizabeth Wakely, A Curse and a Blessing, History Today. Feb. 2013, Vol. 63 Issue 2, p10-16. 7p.
2. Pablo Roitman, Morgan Gilad, Yahel L. E. Ankri and Areih Y. Shalev, Head Injury and Loss of Consciousness Raise the Likelihood of Developing and Maintaining PTSD Symptoms, Journal of Traumatic Stress. Dec. 2013, Vol. 26 Issue 6, p727-734. 8p.

Chapter 2: Embracing Change

1. Michael Scherer, Everett L. Worthington, Joshua N. Hook and Kathryn L. Campana, Forgiveness and the Bottle: Promoting Self-Forgiveness in Individuals Who Abuse Alcohol, Journal of Addictive Disease. Oct-Dec 2011, Vol. 30 Issue 4, p382-395. 14p.
2. Phil E. Miller and Bud Warner, Postdeployment Experiences of Military Mental Health Providers, Military Medicine. Dec 2013, Vol. 178 Issue 12, p1316-1321. 6p.
3. Gayle L. Reed and Robert D. Enright, The Effects of Forgiveness Therapy on Depression, Anxiety,

and Posttraumatic Stress for Women After Spousal Emotional Abuse, Journal of Consulting & Clinical Psychology. Oct 2006, Vol. 74 Issue 5, p920-929. 10p. 3 Charts.

Chapter 3: Enjoying The Journey of Life

1. Cynthia Ricci McCloskey, Changing Focus: Women's Perimenopausal Journey, Health Care for Women International, June 2012, Vol. 33 Issue 6, p540-559. 20p. Copyright © Taylor & Francis Group, LLC.
2. Laura M. Carpenter, Constance A. Nathanson and Young J. Kim, Physical Women, Emotional Men: Gender and Sexual Satisfaction in Midlife, Archives of Sexual Behavior. Feb 2009, Vol. 38 Issue 1, p87-107. 21p. 6 Charts.

Chapter 4: Prioritizing Life

1. Changming Duan, Chris Brown and Chad Keller, Male Counseling Psychologist in Academia: An Exploratory Study of Their Experience in Navigating Career and Family Demands, The Journal of Men's Studies, Vol. 18, No. 3, Fall 2010, 249-267. © 2010 by the Men's Studies Press, LLC. http://www. menstudies.com.
2. Nicky Newton, Cynthia Torges and Abigail Stewart, Women's Regrets About Their Lives: Cohort

Differences in Correlates and Content, Sex Roles. Apr 2012, Vol. 66 Issue 7 / 8, p530-543. 14p.

Chapter 5: Order Out of Chaos

1. Michael Wenzel and Tyler G. Okimoto, How Acts of Forgiveness Restore a Sense of Justice: Addressing Status/Power and Value Concerns Raised by Transgressions, European Journal of Social Psychology Eur. J. Soc. Psuchol. 40, 401-417 (2010) Published online 24 March 2009 in Wiley InterScience (www.interscience.wiley.com) Copyright © 2009 John Wiley & Sons, Ltd.

2. Christianity Today, How Not to Fail Hurting Couples, Christianity Today. 12/14/92, Vol. 36 Issue 15, p35. 3p. Marriage Counseling.

3. William Glasser and Larry L. Palmatier, Marriage Failure: A New Look at an Old Problem, Journal. Oct 96, Vol. 4 Issue 4, p286-298. 13p.

4. Jennifer Montesi, Bradley Connor, Elizabeth Gordon, Kevin Kim and Richard Heimberg, On the Relationship Among Social Anxiety, Intimacy, Sexual Communication and Sexual Satisfaction in Young Couples, Archives of Sexual Behavior. Jan 2013, Vol. 42 Issue 1, p81-91. 11p. 1 Diagram, 1 Chart.

5. Meytal Fisher-Shofty, Yechiel Levkovitz, Simone G. Shamay-Tsoory, Oxytocin Facilitates Accurate

Perception of Competition in Men and Kinship in Women, Social Cognitive & Affective Neuroscience. Mar 2013, Vol. 8 Issue 3, p313-317. 5p.

6. Michael Kosfeld, Markus Heinrichs, Paul J. Zak, Urs Fischbacher and Ernst Fehr, Oxytocin Increase Trust in Humans, Nature. 6/2/2005, Vol. 435 Issue 7042, p673-676. 4p.

7. Sultan Tarlaci, The Brain in Love: Has Neuroscience Stolen the Secret of Love? NeuroQuantology. Dec 2012, Vol. 10 Issue 4, p744-753. 10p.

8. Navneet Magon and Sanjay Kalra, The Orgasmic History of Oxytocin: Love, Lust, and Labor, Indian Journal of Endocrinology & Metabolism. Jul 2011, Supplement 2, pS156-S161. 6p.

Chapter 6: Extracting The Good

1. Ann Macaskill, Defining Forgiveness: Christian Clergy and General Population Perspective, Journal of Personality. Oct 2005, Vol. 73 Issue 5, p1237-1266. 30p. 1 Chart.

2. Paul J. Lim, Matthew Benjamin, Nancy Firor, W. Thomas Smith Jr. and Ingrid Lobet, Digging Your Way Out of Debt, U.S. News & World Report. 03/19/2001, Vol. 130 Issue 11, p52. 8p.

3. Luzolo O. Luzombe and Karol E. Dean, Moderating and Intensifying Factors Influencing Forgiveness by

Priest and Lay People, Pastoral Psychology. Jan 2009, Vol. 57 Issue 5/6, p263-274. 12p.1 Chart.

4. Richard Satran, No More Easy Money, U.S. News Digital Weekly. 8/23/2013, Vol. 5 Issue 34, p25-25. 1p.

5. Heidi Senior, The American Way of Debt, Library Journal. 1/1/2012, Vol. 137 Issue 1, p110-112. 2p. Borrow: The American Way of Debt (Book) by Louis Hyman, Vintage: Random, Jan 2012. c224. p illus.

Chapter 7: Living The Good Life

1. Napa Christie Scollon and Laura A. King, Is The Good Life The Easy Life? Social Indicators Research. Sep 2004, Vol. 68 Issue 2, p127-162. 36p. 2 Charts, 8 Graphs.

2. Sasha Abramsky, The Other America 2012, Nation. 5/14/2012, Vol. 294 Issue 20, p11-18. 6p. 1.

Chapter 8: Experiencing The Abundant Life

1. Stephen T. Fife, Gerald R. Weeks and Jessica Stellberg-Filbert, Facilitating Forgiveness in the Treatment of Infidelity: An Interpersonal Model, Journal of Family Therapy. Nov 2013, Vol. 35 Issue 4, p343-367. 25p. 1 Chart.

2. Edward T. Pound and Gary Cohen, Living Well is The Best Revenge, U.S. News & World Report, 00415537, 6/7/93, Vol. 114 Issue 22, p30. 1p.

3. The Greek words[1],[2] are taken from the Strong's Complete Word Study Concordance: Expanded Edition, Edited by Warren Baker. James Strong, LL.D., S.T.D. Copyright © 2004 by AMG Publishers, 6815 Shallowford Rd., Chattanooga, TN 37421. Used by permission. All rights reserved.

Chapter 9: The Authentic Good

1. Vickie Bane, Forgiving My Father, People. 3/28/2011, Vol. 75 Issue 12, p107-108. 2p. 3. Copyright © Time Inc. 2011. The Source of All Things: A Memoir, The (Book) by Tracy Ross.
2. Mark Galli, Incredible Journeys, Christianity Today. Dec 2012, Vol. 56 Issue 11, p24-30. 7p.

ABOUT THE AUTHOR

L oretta R. McIntosh is a prolific inspirational and motivational conference speaker and host. She is a visionary, a mentor, a life coach, and a business-woman. Throughout her nearly thirty-four years of leadership and public speaking, Dr. McIntosh has trained numerous leaders and has administered healing to the masses throughout America and in many parts of the world. For a period of more than four years, her message of hope beamed into millions of homes in over a hundred foreign nations via her weekly television, satellite, and short-wave radio broadcasts. Today, she serves as the executive producer and host of her Web TV Broadcast. She is the author of several books, including *The Eviction* and *Healing The Hurt,* and continues to be in global demand as a speaker. She is the founder, president, and CEO of Impartations, Inc., a multi-faceted non-profit organization headquartered in Frisco, Texas, with outreaches in other locations, dedicated to reaching the lost, the hungry, and the destitute worldwide. Her blog can be read at GetTheGoodOutOfLife.com. She can be followed at Twitter.com/DrLMcIntosh.

Dear Friend,

You are cordially invited to join us at the Get The Good Out Of Life book lounge at www.getthegoodoutoflife.com. This is a social gathering place for learning and a place where the thoughts: *you can become…*and *you are becoming…*merge and create *a successful new you!*

This connection could be the beginning of something fresh and new for you; a time of new discoveries in life and a season of advancement. But you will never know what lies ahead without venturing into new territory, and positing and planting yourself for new growth and development.

The challenge will be to extract the good out of life when it seems no good can be found, because good often remains hidden behind the walls of pain and suffering. You will be amazed at how beautiful and fragrant life can be as you search for good and find it.

Those who anticipate the good will no doubt receive it.

Life is as good as gold,

Loretta McIntosh

www.getthegoodoutoflife.com

Get The Good Out Of Life

The Book Lounge

People of all ages spend innumerable hours on the Internet, most of which can be very tiring. Why not join us at your leisure at www.getthegoodoutoflife.com for a relaxing social hour or two?

Through this form of social media, you can have a cup of mocha and unwind from a hard day's work, find quite time on a vacation, or make time anytime to join us at our online *book lounge*.

This is the gathering place for book lovers to slip away from it all and journey to places far beyond the imagination. And it's a place that will empower you to dream, to believe, and to live again.

You will be refreshed and inspired as you catch up on the latest insightful messages and chapter readings of additional books by author Loretta McIntosh; you'll also be able to communicate your questions, as well as share your thoughts.

CPSIA information can be obtained at www.ICGtesting.com
Printed in the USA
LVOW13*1508070514

384804LV00002B/15/P